*Also available in this series (titles listed by syllabus section):*

**ATYPICAL DEVELOPMENT AND ABNORMAL BEHAVIOUR**

**Psychopathology**
*John D. Stirling and Jonathan S.E. Hellewell*

**Therapeutic Approaches in Psychology**
*Susan Cave*

**Classification and Diagnosis of Abnormal Psychology**
*Susan Cave (forthcoming)*

**BIO-PSYCHOLOGY**

**Cortical Functions**
*John Stirling*

**The Physiological Basis of Behaviour: Neural and hormonal processes**
*Kevin Silber*

**Awareness: Biorhythms, sleep and dreaming**
*Evie Bentley*

**COGNITIVE PSYCHOLOGY**

**Memory and Forgetting**
*John Henderson*

**Perception: Theory, development and organisation**
*Paul Rookes and Jane Willson*

**Attention and Pattern Recognition**
*Nick Lund*

**DEVELOPMENTAL PSYCHOLOGY**

**Early Socialisation: Sociability and attachment**
*Cara Flanagan*

**Social and Personality Development**
*Tina Abbott*

**PERSPECTIVES AND RESEARCH**

**Controversies in Psychology**
*Philip Banyard*

**Ethical Issues and Guidelines in Psychology**
*Cara Flanagan and Philip Banyard*

**Introducing Research and Data in Psychology: A guide to methods and analysis**
*Ann Searle*

**Theoretical Approaches in Psychology**
*Matt Jarvis*

**Debates in Psychology**
*Andy Bell (forthcoming)*

**SOCIAL PSYCHOLOGY**

**Social Influences**
*Kevin Wren*

**Interpersonal Relationships**
*Diana Dwyer*

**Social Cognition**
*Donald C. Pennington*

**COMPARATIVE PSYCHOLOGY**

**Determinants of Animal Behaviour**
*JoAnne Cartwright (forthcoming)*

**Evolutionary Explanations of Human Behaviour**
*John Cartwright (forthcoming)*

**OTHER TITLES**

**Sport Psychology**
*Matt Jarvis*

**Psychology and Work**
*Christine Hodson (forthcoming)*

**Psychology and Education**
*Susan Bentham (forthcoming)*

**Psychology and Crime**
*David Putwain and Aidan Sammons (forthcoming)*

**STUDY GUIDE**

**Exam Success in AQA(A) Psychology**
*Paul Humphreys (forthcoming)*

To my family for their continued support and
encouragement, and to Copper for keeping
me healthy!

# Health Psychology

*Anthony J. Curtis*

First published 2000
by Routledge
11 New Fetter Lane, London EC4P 4EE

Simultaneously published in the USA and Canada
by Routledge
29 West 35th Street, New York, NY 10001

Reprinted 2001
by Routledge
27 Church Road, Hove, East Sussex BN3 2FA

*Routledge is an imprint of the Taylor & Francis Group*

© 2000 Anthony J. Curtis

Typeset in Times and Frutiger by Keystroke,
Jacaranda Lodge, Wolverhampton
Printed and bound in Great Britain by
TJ International Ltd, Padstow, Cornwall

*British Library Cataloguing in Publication Data*
A catalogue record for this book is available from the British Library

*Library of Congress Cataloging in Publication Data*
Curtis, Anthony J. (Anthony James), 1963–
  Health Psychology / Anthony J. Curtis.
      p. cm. – (Routledge modular psychology)
    Includes bibliographical references and index.
    ISBN 0–415–19272–2 (hb). – ISBN 0–415–19273–0 (pb)
    1. Clinical health psychology.   2. Medicine and psychology.
  3. Health—Psychological aspects.    I. Title.   II. Series.
  R726.7.C88      1999                                    99-32420
  613'.01'9—dc21                                              CIP

ISBN 0–415–19272–2 (hbk)
ISBN 0–415–19273–0 (pbk)

# Contents

# Illustrations

**Figures**

**Tables**

# Acknowledgements

I would like to sincerely thank, first and foremost, Cara Flanagan and Kevin Silber for their support, encouragement and humour throughout the writing of this text. Their dedication and commitment to the task was both motivating and inspiring. I would also like to thank Moira Taylor and Alison Dixon at Routledge for their advice, support and encouragement throughout the stages of drafting, editing and production. Their expertise, patience and general assistance with this text have contributed significantly to ensure its final delivery. Thanks also go to Paul Humphreys, Phil Banyard and Dave Clarke for their comments, advice and assistance with the Study Aids chapter. Particular thanks also go to Prof. Marian Pitts and Dr Karen Legge for their helpful and constructive reviews.

I would also like to thank my colleagues and students at Bath Spa University College for their support and encouragement throughout the writing of this text. Finally, I would like to thank my family for their continued support and inspiration.

Anthony J. Curtis and Routledge acknowledge OCR (Oxford, Cambridge and RSA examinations) for permission to use their examination material. The OCR bears no responsibility for the example answers taken from its past papers which are contained in this publication.

Every effort has been made to trace copyright holders and obtain permission to reproduce figures and tables. Any omissions brought to our attention will be remedied in future editions.

# Introduction to health psychology

Welcome to the fascinating area of health psychology! This text aims to provide an insight into the many fields that make up health psychology. You may be a student, nurse or other practitioner in the health field, or just seeking to find out more about your health and the role that psychology can play in understanding health states and health status. I hope that this book is of interest to you and relevant to your needs.

## Defining health psychology

In trying to define **health psychology**, one must first try and define what is meant by 'health' as a concept. The most commonly quoted definition of health is provided in the Constitution of the World Health Organization (WHO, 1946):

Health is a state of complete physical, mental and social well-being, and not merely the absence of disease or infirmity.

This definition is considered to have positive and negative attributes by Downie *et al.* (1996). In the first part of the definition, they argue that health is seen in positive terms (i.e. the *presence* of a positive quality: well-being). In the second part of the definition, health is viewed (in a negative sense) as involving the *absence* of disease or infirmity (themselves negative in connotation). Taken together, the definition implies that true health involves both a prevention of ill-health (e.g. disease, injury, illness) and the promotion of positive health, the latter of which has been largely neglected.

Banyard (1996) has criticised the above definition on the grounds that a state of *complete* physical, mental and social well-being is very difficult to achieve in reality and that the definition ignores wider social, political and economic factors which may contribute to this state. It further implies that people who are not fulfilled are also not healthy!

## Historical perspective on health and illness

From the seventeenth century to the beginning of the twentieth century, most people in Western society considered that ill-health was something that just 'happened to someone' and that there was very little that could be done in terms of protecting against it. Once they were ill, it was argued, people simply expected to seek medical care in order to be cured. Unfortunately, medicine was not always able to help them. In fact, the leading causes of death during this period were the **acute** (i.e. sudden-onset) infectious diseases such as influenza, pneumonia and tuberculosis. Once contracted, the duration of such illnesses was relatively short: a person either died or got well within a matter of weeks. People also felt little responsibility for contracting these illnesses because they believed that it was impossible to avoid them. Some believed that their illness was the work of evil forces or divine intervention.

Today, the major causes of disease and illness are very different. They are the **chronic** (i.e. slow-onset, long-term) 'diseases of living', especially heart disease, cancer and **diabetes**. These are the main contributors to disability and death and usually cannot be 'cured' (unlike the traditional infectious diseases) but rather must be managed by patients and their doctors. This dramatic shift in the causes (and consequences) of illness, disease and mortality reflects not only our increased understanding of medicine but also demands new methods of treatment. Also, as patterns of illness have changed over time, so has our need for new models of health.

The generally held view is that, with rapid developments in medical technology and interventions, infectious diseases such as tuberculosis, measles and chicken pox have dramatically declined as a consequence of the introduction of chemotherapy and vaccinations. Similarly, the use of antibiotics was believed to be responsible for the dramatic decline in the incidence and prevalence of pneumonia and flu. There appears therefore to be a clear relationship between a specific **pathogen** (disease-causing organism) and a physical illness. This is the view held by the **biomedical model** which has dominated medicine and health psychology until recently.

## The biomedical model

The biomedical model (or 'medical model' as it is also known) takes the view that there are known and knowable physical causes for disorders. Specifically, germs, genes and chemicals may all contribute in different ways to the causes of disorders. Subsequent treatments are usually also based on physical interventions (e.g. medicines, surgery, etc.). The roots of this approach date back to the seventeenth century and **Cartesian dualism**, when Western science made a clear distinction between mind and body. The famous French philosopher René Descartes proposed that mind and body are separate entities, rather like a ghost and a biological machine. Different versions of dualism since Descartes have sought to explain the relationship between mind and body, some seeing one as influencing the other and vice versa. According to Descartes, the seat of the soul was in the pineal gland located in the brain and he also believed that animals did not possess such a soul. Modern Western medicine, however, is not dualist and instead is firmly rooted in a monist (materialist) philosophy.

Historically, philosophers have vacillated between the view that the mind and the body are part of the same system and the idea that they are two separate ones. The Greeks developed a humoral theory of illness that was first proposed by Hippocrates in the fourth century BC and expanded by Galen over 500 years later. According to the Greeks, disease arises when the four creating fluids of the body (blood, black bile, yellow bile and phlegm) are out of balance.

Treatment involved restoring this balance among the humours and a predominance of one humour was associated with specific bodily temperaments. The important notion here is that disease states were linked to bodily factors (i.e. the later medical model) although these factors could also influence the mind (i.e. the later **biopsychosocial model**). The Middle Ages saw a swing back to mental explanations of illness (e.g. mysticism and demonology dominated concepts of disease) and this was seen as God's punishment for wrongdoing. Cure or relief was sought through driving out the evil by torturing the body. Penance and good works thankfully replaced this 'therapy'! Even today, the links between mind and body, and between religion and healing, remain very close.

EVALUATION OF THE BIOMEDICAL MODEL

- This approach has been criticised for being reductionist in approach (e.g. reducing explanations of illness to explanations involving germs, genes and/or chemicals when wider social and economic factors may also be responsible). One of the main features of **holistic** medicine is to consider the whole person in treatment and not simply the diseased part of their body.
- Another criticism of the biomedical model is that it often assumes physical causes for disorders. Many 'modern' disorders described above (e.g. heart disease, cancer, diabetes, etc.) are considered to be 'multi-factorial' disorders; that is, they have many potential causes which may often interact with one another. For example, heart disease may be a product of genetic factors, diet and lifestyle/ behaviour factors, each playing a role in terms of susceptibility to illness, management and treatment success. We have at last acknowledged that humans are not simply machines operating in a social and economic vacuum but rather we are dynamic individuals with many thoughts, feelings and emotions. The extent to which these are merely activities of the brain is still heavily debated.
- Finally, the biomedical model is criticised for placing too much emphasis on 'body' at the expense of 'mind' as distinguished above. The problem here is that a growing body of research evidence, and indeed our own experiences of health and illness, suggests that our mind influences our body and vice versa. We constantly read of a

cancer patient's 'will' in managing cancer and the role of **cognitive-behaviour therapy** in treating a whole range of disorders. Although the mechanisms linking mind and body are not well understood, many health professionals now believe there is a link and that the absence of evidence should not be taken as evidence of absence.

## The biopsychosocial model

During the last quarter of the twentieth century, physicians, psychologists and medical sociologists have seriously questioned the usefulness of the medical model in explaining health and illness. The **biopsychosocial** model (see Figure 1.1) is based on a systems approach. At one end of this scale, as Banyard (1996) states, we exist within an ecological system that includes the planet we live on, the life we have developed from and the species we are part of. At the other end of the scale, we are made up of the basic units of the universe (molecules, atoms, etc.). There are no single causes in explaining phenomena here. Instead, many factors influence each other on different levels.

In applying this model to health psychology, there has been an increasing need to recognise these additional and wider factors that may affect our health. Engel (1977) proposed a biopsychosocial model

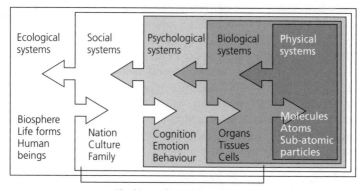

The biopsychosocial model

*Figure 1.1* **The biopsychosocial model**

*Source:* Originally titled 'Systems' in P. Banyard (1996, p. 6) with permission from Hodder & Stoughton Educational.

of health, which considered that a person's health was the result of an interaction of biological (i.e. biomedical), psychological and social factors. In other words, biological factors (e.g. viruses, bacteria and lesions) interact with psychological factors (e.g. attitudes, beliefs, behaviours) and social factors (e.g. class, employment, ethnicity) to determine one's health (see Chapter 2). Similarly, psychological interventions have been effective in the treatment of pain (Chapter 4); cancer, coronary heart disease (CHD) and HIV/AIDS (Chapter 6); and stress (Chapter 8).

**Progress exercise**

Think back to the last time that you were unwell or ill. Can you think of biological, psychological and social factors that may have contributed to this? List them in a table using these three categories:

Biological factors        Psychological factors        Social factors

### Social and environmental factors

We have now widened up the topic of health and illness to consider other factors that affect our health status. The view that social and environmental factors impact on our health was also supported by Thomas McKeown (1979) in his book *The Role of Medicine*. McKeown examined the impact of medicine on health from the seventeenth century onwards and found, quite remarkably, that the reduction in infectious diseases such as tuberculosis, pneumonia and influenza was already under way *before* the development of medical interventions. Further, he argued that these reductions would have taken place anyway because of improvements in social and environmental factors. He argued that:

> The influences which led to [the] predominance [of infectious diseases] from the time of the first agricultural revolution 10,000 years ago were insufficient food, environmental hazards and excessive numbers and the measures which led to their decline from the time of the modern Agricultural and Industrial

revolutions were predictably improved nutrition, better hygiene and contraception.

(McKeown, 1979, p. 17, cited in Ogden, 1996, p. 12)

It is impossible to tell therefore whether health improvements of the nineteenth century were due to medicine, social and economic factors or, probably, all of these factors working together. What remains the challenge today for health psychologists is to use these insights to help manage the modern-day threats to our health: the 'problems of living'. With modern increases in life-expectancy, dramatic changes in working practices and associated healthy lifestyles, the view now is that health is a valued and valuable resource which we all possess and that, through careful management and healthy behaviours, we can all enjoy the good things in life that much longer.

### A new model of health

As a way of resolving some of these problems, and of viewing health as a relative rather than an absolute concept, Downie *et al.* (1996) proposed a new model of health, illustrated in Figure 1.2. In considering the area of positive health, Downie *et al.* (1996) used the concept of 'true well-being' rather than subjective well-being because the latter may be deceptive, arising from influences that are overall detrimental to an individual's functioning (e.g. drug-induced euphoria) or to society in general. Instead, Downie *et al.* believe that true well-being reflects a process of being empowered with having a 'good life'. For example, having friends, satisfaction of material needs, having control of one's life, being able to choose what one wants to do or be and being able to develop one's talents, and having the autonomy to develop and express these qualities. All of these qualities go to make up our true well-being.

Downie *et al.* state that positive health also encompasses the notion of 'fitness'. This concept focuses on physical attributes of health, and can be summarised as the four S's: Strength, Stamina, Suppleness and Skills. These qualities allow us to perform routine, everyday tasks, without suffering undue physical discomfort (e.g. muscle aches) or perform highly specialised roles or tasks. Fitness is seen here as a means to an end (i.e. positive health) rather than an end in itself, although this may not always be the case. Furthermore,

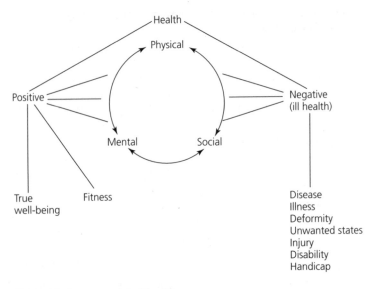

**Figure 1.2 A new model of health**

*Source*: Originally titled 'A Model of Health' in Downie *et al*. (1996, p. 24) *Health Promotion: Models and Values* by permission of Oxford University Press.

feelings of fitness may not necessarily result in feelings of well-being. This area will be considered in more detail in Chapter 7.

To sum up, the whole idea of the new model of health is to extend the WHO (1946) definition of health, and to redress the imbalance between positive and negative health. This is achieved by promoting positive health and using **health promotion** as the vehicle to achieve the balanced enhancement of physical, mental and social positive health, together with the prevention of physical, mental and social ill-health.

EVALUATION OF THE NEW MODEL OF HEALTH (DOWNIE ET AL., 1996)

This model allows for positive and negative dimensions of health, each being interconnected with the physical, mental and social elements from the above WHO (1946) definition. The model also reinforces the idea that these elements of our health often go hand in hand. If we suffer from physical illness, for example, a low level of well-being may also accompany this.

On the negative (ill-health) side of the above model, Downie *et al.* (1996) perhaps controversially include a wide range of examples expressed in terms of physically abnormal conditions (e.g. disease, deformity) and/or unwanted conditions (e.g. skin rashes) and/or incapacitating conditions (e.g. injuries to limbs). These may not necessarily be directly connected to ill-health. Downie *et al.* also argue that positive and negative health have interconnected physical, mental and social elements, although the exact relationship between these areas remains unclear.

## Psychology and health

The role of psychology in the prevention, management and promotion of our health has emerged as one of the most exciting and challenging tasks of the twentieth century. The establishment of **Health Psychology** as Division 38 within the American Psychological Association (APA) in 1978 and, more recently, being awarded Division status within the British Psychological Society (BPS), reflects the increasing need and value of applying insights in psychology to health and health-care outcomes (Matarazzo, 1994).

Within the last ten years, health psychology has contributed to identifying individual behaviours and lifestyles that affect a person's physical health, the prevention and treatment of illness, identifying risk factors associated with ill-health, improving health-care systems through identifying good practice and shaping public opinion with regard to people's health.

The application of psychological principles to the health field has also contributed to a range of positive and successful outcomes, including the lowering of **high blood pressure** and controlling **cholesterol** levels. It has also been involved in managing stress, alleviating pain, reducing and stopping smoking and moderating other risky behaviours (e.g. alcohol intake). In the area of health promotion, health psychologists have been involved in encouraging regular exercise, medical and dental check-ups and practising 'safer' behaviours (e.g. by encouraging 'safe sex').

As can be seen in Figure 1.3 below, health psychology overlaps with many other health-related fields and disciplines. We can see that health psychology works together with many other fields and disciplines, preventing ill-health and promoting health and well-being.

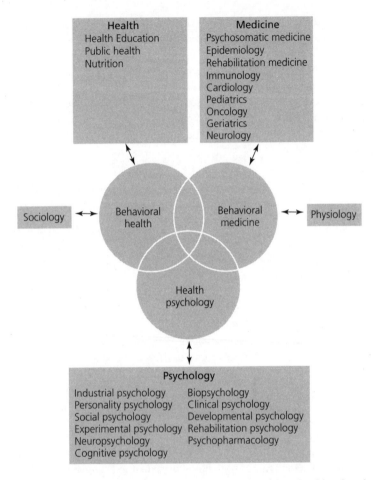

**Figure 1.3 Relationship of health psychology to other health-related fields**

*Source*: From *Health Psychology: An Introduction to Behavior and Health, 3/e, 3rd edition*, by L. Brannon and J. Feist. © 1997. Reprinted with permission of Wadsworth Publishing, a division of International Thomson Publishing. Fax 800 730-2215.

## Models of behaviour change

Before we look at some of the major models of behaviour change in health psychology, it is worth considering for a moment that models are no more than descriptions of how something (e.g. a process) *might* work rather than an explanation of how something actually *does* work. In other words, models are best guesses about what factors, on their own or in combination, predict behaviour change. They are not solutions in themselves to understanding human behaviour and experience. Instead, they provide us with a window into those factors that might be operating here. Further, such models may then be used to predict behaviour change or design successful health intervention strategies.

Most of the models of behaviour change in health psychology are called 'social–cognitive models' because, as their name suggests, they focus on the social context of behaviour change (e.g. situational cues) and cognitive processes (e.g. perception, memory). It is the interaction of social and cognitive factors that determines the likelihood for behaviour change.

These models also differ in terms of whether they describe motivational/emotional aspects and/or behavioural aspects of our behaviour. Some models also recognise that there may be different stages we go through in changing our behaviour. As we can already see, models of behaviour change can get quite elaborate with many different variables to consider. You are asked to see the further reading section at the end of this chapter for texts containing detailed descriptions of each model. For the purpose of this chapter, I will contrast the most well-known and earliest cognitive model of behaviour change, the **health belief model (HBM)** (Rosenstock, 1966) with an action maintenance (or stages of change) model (Prochaska and DiClemente, 1982). This is to show how each model focuses on a different feature of behaviour change.

### The health belief model (HBM)

The health belief model was developed initially by Rosenstock (1966) and further by Becker and colleagues throughout the 1970s and 1980s to predict preventive health behaviours and responses to treatments in patients who were acutely and chronically ill (Ogden, 1996). It is illustrated in Figure 1.4.

This model suggests that the likelihood that an individual will engage in a given health behaviour (e.g. smoking) will depend on:

- perceived internal cues (e.g. breathlessness) and/or external cues (e.g. information leaflets on smoking)
- perceived susceptibility (e.g. my chances of getting lung cancer are high if I smoke)
- perceived severity (lung cancer is a serious illness)
- perceived benefits (if I stop smoking, I will have more money to spend on other things)
- perceived costs (stopping smoking will make me irritable)

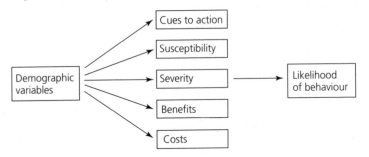

*Figure 1.4* **Basics of the health belief model**
*Source*: J. Ogden (1996, p. 21) with permission from Open University Press.

These core beliefs act together in determining how likely we are to act. Notice that perceptions play a crucial role here and therefore we may not be objective in making these assessments.

EVALUATION OF THE HEALTH BELIEF MODEL

- Although the HBM has been successfully used to predict, for example, cancer screening behaviour in women (Murray and McMillan, 1993), there have been conflicting findings. Some studies have found, for example, that healthy behaviour is more strongly related to low susceptibility (e.g. taking exercise to reduce the risk of heart disease), not high susceptibility, as the model would predict.
- The model appears to ignore social and environmental factors affecting our health (discussed earlier in this chapter).
- The model, like other models, assumes that humans process information and behave in a rational manner. Evidence suggests

that this may not be the case. Humans are rationalising (after the event!) rather than rational agents of behaviour change.

- More recent models have found stronger predictors of behaviour change such as outcome expectancies (how likely I am to be successful) and **self-efficacy** (perceived confidence in being able to achieve a particular behaviour change).
- This model has, however, provided a useful working model on which to base subsequent more advanced models and has stimulated much valuable research into behaviour change.

### *The stages of change model*

This model is sometimes known as the 'transtheoretical model of behaviour change' because it brought together eighteen different treatments in order to understand the changes that people go through in bringing about and maintaining change. The idea here is that individuals go through five different stages (see Figure 1.5) in changing their health behaviour:

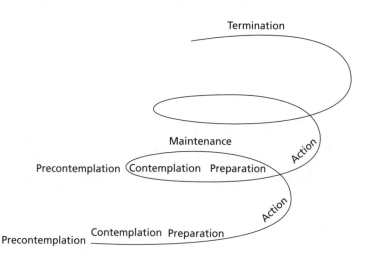

***Figure 1.5*** **Stages of change model**

*Source*: Originally titled 'The spiral model of change proposed by Prochaska et al.', Prochaska *et al*. Copyright © 1992 by the American Psychological Association. Reprinted with permission.

Stage 1: Precontemplation (not intending to make any changes)
Stage 2: Contemplation (considering a change)
Stage 3: Preparation (making small changes)
Stage 4: Action: (actively engaging in new behaviour)
Stage 5: Maintenance (sustaining the change over time)

We may start anywhere on this spiral of stages (depending on what behaviours we are changing) and we may even go backwards during some changes (e.g. an individual may temporarily slip back to the contemplation stage after reaching the maintenance stage).

EVALUATION OF THE STAGES OF CHANGE MODEL

- This model has been successfully applied to several health-related behaviours including smoking cessation, reduction in alcohol intake, exercise and cancer screening behaviour (e.g. DiClemente *et al.*, 1991; Marcus *et al.*, 1992).
- This model goes further than the HBM model by recognising the importance of the passage of time involved in behaviour change and allowing individuals to focus on different rewards and costs at each stage.
- The stages of change model is a dynamic model that links behaviour health goals to the stages and processes that people move through in trying to bring about long-term behaviour change. This may be the case for example in treating addictions (e.g. smoking, alcohol, etc.) and the model allows for specific interventions to be designed around these stages.
- It may, however, be difficult to recognise the particular stage that an individual may be in. In a review of the literature, Prochaska *et al.* (1992) found that only 10–15 per cent of addicted smokers were prepared for action. Most were in the precontemplative and contemplative stages. It seems that problem health behaviour is not perceived as a problem to those who are most at risk!

## *Comparing the models*

Pitts and Phillips (1998) argue that there remains a clear need for further empirical research that tests these and other models so that determinants of precautionary health behaviours can be identified. In addition, health interventions can then be designed to suit particular types of health conditions so that attitudes, beliefs and behaviours change as a result of such initiatives. We know more about the causes of illness, disease and 'health-risking' behaviours than we do about preventive health behaviours, and health psychology continues to move towards addressing this latter area. The above models, together with other models of health, share the view that perceived risk, perceived severity of the disease, perceived effectiveness of the precautions, social norms, self-efficacy and cost–benefit analysis are all important predictors of preventive health behaviours (Pitts and Phillips, 1998). We must now not only work towards establishing which of these factors are most important for particular health conditions, but also examine how or in what ways these factors inter-act with each other in influencing our health conditions and health behaviours. One example of implementing such research findings into practice, the need to promote **testicular self-examination** in men as a preventive measure against testicular cancer, is considered below.

*Case study: Changing behaviour in men: testicular self-examination*

Testicular cancer is not only the most common cancer in men, but also one of the leading causes of death in men, between the ages of 15 and 35 years. Moreover, its incidence appears to be increasing (National Cancer Institute, 1987). Testicular cancer is also a preventable cause of premature death and so merits intervention. Remarkably, very few men know what the symptoms to look out for are, what the procedures for screening are, or what the prognosis for recovery is (entirely cur-able if detected in its early stages). This is in direct contrast to breast cancer screening in women where most women are fully aware and informed of such procedures (see Chapter 9 for an example).

Effective testicular self-examination (TSE) is quite similar to effective **breast self-examination**. It involves becoming familiar with the surface, texture and consistency of the testicles, examination during a warm bath or shower, and examination of both testicles rotated between the thumb and forefinger to determine that the entire surface is free of lumps (Hongladrom and Hongladrom, 1982). Few studies have designed interventions to assess the effectiveness of TSE although Friman *et al.* (1986 cited in Taylor, 1995) provided young men with a brief check-list of TSE skills and found that such an educational intervention dramatically increased confidence in reporting symptoms of TSE. A follow-up study by telephone found that this skill had been continued long after the intervention. In addition, men reported that they were more likely to practise TSE because they believed they were reducing their risks of cancer and that others would approve of this screening behaviour (subjective norms).

## Summary

We have seen in this chapter that health and illness are difficult concepts to define. Health is now seen by many as a valued resource that can extend one's lifespan and improve the quality of one's well-being and overall **quality of life**. The emphasis on health promotion rather than disease prevention is recognised as we move into the twenty-first century. It has been shown here that, although models of preventive health behaviour share certain features in predicting behaviour, different models of health have emphasised different factors that are considered to influence behaviour change. Earlier models are now being revised or even replaced by more sophisticated models which claim to predict behaviour change more accurately. What is increasingly important here is the role of *perceived* factors (e.g. risk, rewards, costs, etc.) rather than *actual* risks, rewards and costs. As a result, social–cognitive models have emphasised these factors and transactional models have further placed these factors within a dynamic, active health context. Taken together, these models suggest that humans are thinking, feeling, rationalising (not always rational!) individuals who enjoy and value many things in life, one of which is their health.

One recent extension of how individuals may rationalise their 'risky behaviours' in a biased manner is the notion of **unrealistic optimism** (Weinstein, 1984). This phenomenon suggests that some individuals ignore their own risk-increasing behaviour ('I may not always practise safe sex') and focus instead on their risk-reducing behaviour ('but at least I don't inject drugs'). This results in individuals' engaging in a 'selective focus' of perceived risks and susceptibility, which may not necessarily be rational. Health psychology has had notable success in changing problem or risky behaviours by designing interventions and strategies around these theoretical models and assumptions. However, future models of behaviour change will need to further consider the role of individual differences in behaviour and recognise that the sequence of decision making and decision taking may not necessarily be logical and rational.

## Further reading

Descriptions and evaluation of the major models of behaviour change can be found in the textbooks as summarised in Table 1.1. All of these textbooks provide very good descriptions and evaluations of these models and show how they have been successfully applied to the prevention, promotion, intervention and maintenance of a range of health conditions and behaviours.

**Table 1.1** Major models of behaviour change

| Model of behaviour change | | Textbooks |
|---|---|---|
| 1 | Health belief model | A B C D |
| 2 | Protection motivation theory | A B C |
| 3 | Theory of reasoned action | C D |
| 4 | Theory of planned behaviour | A B C D |
| 5 | Health action process approach | A B |
| 6 | Spontaneous processing model | C |

Key:
A: Ogden, J. (1996) *Health Psychology: A Textbook*, Buckingham: Open University Press.
B: Pitts, M. and Phillips, K. (eds) (1998) *The Psychology of Health: An introduction*, 2nd edn, London: Routledge.
C: Stroebe, W. and Stroebe, M. (1995) *Social Psychology and Health*, Buckingham: Open University Press.
D: Taylor, S. E. (1995) *Health Psychology*, 3rd edn, New York: McGraw-Hill.

# 2

# Social epidemiology and health policy

What is epidemiology?
Mortality and morbidity
Quality of life
Health policy
Summary

Health psychologists are interested in the study of health for both individuals and whole populations. As we saw in the previous chapter, changing patterns of health over time and place have allowed researchers to study trends that may inform them about the particular pattern of disease or illness. This may be useful in terms of designing interventions which may, for example, arrest specific diseases before they have a chance to have a dramatic effect on a population. Further, in well-planned health economies, we may prevent the initial onset of a disease by, for example, immunising an entire population or those considered most at risk (e.g. influenza injections for the young and elderly).

## What is epidemiology?

**Epidemiology** is closely related to health psychology in its goals and interests. It is defined as the study of the frequency, distribution and causes of infectious and non-infectious disease in a population, based on an investigation of the physical and social environment (Taylor,

**19**

1995, p. 9). As such, epidemiology focuses on populations rather than specific individuals, and the trends that such populations show allow us to make certain predictions about the relative likelihood of contracting a specific disease or illness. In addition, epidemiologists not only consider who has what kind of cancer, but also seek to answer questions such as why some cancers are more prevalent in particular geographic areas than others are.

The first known epidemiological investigation was conducted in 1849 by an English doctor, John Snow, who observed that the London cholera epidemic occurred mainly in the areas that were served by the Broad Street Water Pump. After the pump was closed the epidemic subsided, thus exposing the source of the epidemic. Modern epidemiologists are still focused on finding the causes of diseases although today's problems are often more difficult to detect and may involve more factors operating together. For example, a previously unknown micro-organism called *Legionella pneumophila* was found to be responsible for an outbreak of respiratory disease at an American Legion Convention in Philadelphia in 1976. Similarly, another new disease entity which was discovered four years later in 1980 was toxic shock syndrome, a potentially fatal infection with staphylococcal bacteria that was found to be associated with the use of tampons in menstruating women. Both diseases were identified by epidemiologists working for the Epidemiological Intelligence Service for the Centers for Disease Control (CDC), which is the main epidemiological unit based in Atlanta, USA. The CDC is still the main intelligence centre for such disease outbreaks and is regularly consulted by the UK's Department of Health.

Unlike the clear-cut causation usually found between micro-organisms and infectious diseases, epidemiological investigations into chronic diseases such as heart disease and cancer are often less conclusive. The links between genetic, biological, psychological and social factors, and their role in the onset and treatment of chronic diseases like heart disease and cancer, remains one of the greatest challenges facing epidemiologists today.

## Mortality and morbidity

Epidemiologists use specific terms to describe and summarise the above patterns or trends. For example, **morbidity** refers to the number of cases of a disease that exist at some given point in time. This may be further broken down in terms of the number of new cases (incidence) or as the total number of existing cases (prevalence) as shown in Figure 2.1. In summary, morbidity statistics tell us how many people are suffering from what kinds of illnesses at any given time. To complement these numbers, **mortality** refers to the numbers of deaths due to particular causes (rather than disease or illness) as shown by, for example, Figure 2.2 which gives death rates for the ten leading causes of death per 100,000 population in the USA (1900 vs. 1990).

Measures of morbidity and mortality are essential tools for designing, implementing and evaluating a range of health-care policies and

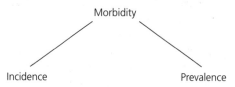

*Figure 2.1* **Morbidity and mortality**

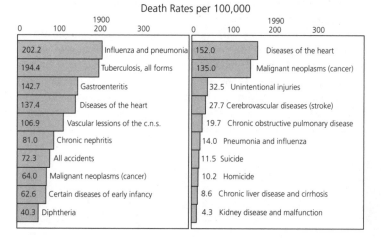

*Figure 2.2* **Death rates for the ten leading causes of death per 100, 000 population, United States, 1900 and 1990**

*Source*: From *Health Psychology*, 3rd edn by S. E. Taylor © 1995. Reprinted with permission of The McGraw-Hill Companies.

practices. We need to understand the frequency and distribution of illness, disease and death rates, and the causes that underlie them. As a result, we can minimise or eradicate the causes of disease and illness and reduce the risks of early death. For example, knowing that car accidents have historically been one of the major causes of death in children, adolescents and young adults has led to a range of positive safety initiatives, including child safety seats, mandatory seat-belt laws and airbags. Similarly, knowing that cardiac disease is the major cause of premature death in the UK and the USA has led to a range of health-promoting and protecting initiatives (e.g. dietary changes, smoking cessation programmes).

The need to consider both mortality and morbidity is extremely important here. We must not only consider how to prevent deaths but also how to improve illness and disease states as well. Both of these challenges are relevant to modern-day health states since chronic illnesses (i.e. long-term diseases that cannot be cured, only managed) are the main contributors to both disability and death. For example, heart disease, cancer and diabetes are complex multi-factorial conditions (i.e. many factors may contribute to their causes and treatments, including genetic and environmental factors) and we now know that psychological and social factors are involved at all stages of the development of these disorders.

This contrasts sharply with traditional causes of death at the turn of the last century (e.g. influenza, pneumonia and tuberculosis) where, once contracted, the prognosis for recovery was often very limited (see Chapter 1). Indeed, one could argue that, such is the nature of modern-day health disorders, 'most (if not all!) deaths are to some extent "suicides" in the sense that they could have been postponed if more resources had been invested in prolonging life' (Becker, 1976, pp. 10–11).

**Progress exercise**

Consider the introduction of mandatory seat-belt laws and no-smoking areas in public places in this country. In each case, how should we balance the criticism of introducing a 'nanny-state' approach to controlling other people's behaviour as opposed to a 'victim-blaming' or even a 'laissez-faire' (complete freedom) approach? Are the health needs of the population more important than the freedom of the individual?

### Research into morbidity and mortality

A large-scale epidemiological study into factors affecting morbidity and mortality found that social and environmental factors were as important as an individual's lifestyle in promoting health and preventing early death (see Chapter 7 on lifestyles and health). Hart, (cited in Holland *et al.*, 1991) recorded that Tokyo is one of the world's largest, most polluted and congested cities, yet it has the lowest infant mortality and longest life expectancy of any place on earth! The reason Hart gives for this is that social engineering in Tokyo has created a synthetic environment that is made by and for human beings. He explodes the myth that life in a state of nature is more wholesome and healthy than life in an industrial society. Indeed, clues from palaeolithic demography suggest that the body of industrial man was twice as durable as that of his stone age ancestor! (Roosevelt, 1984 cited in Holland *et al.*, 1991). Hart goes on to describe how social and economic factors, including economic and social institutions (e.g. marriage, family, law, etc.) work together to enhance this durability, whilst also regulating relationships and protecting the rights of every citizen.

In addition, countries with poorly managed social and economic conditions also have high morbidity and mortality rates. For example, modern-day Hungary may experience a relatively high standard of living, but non-material forces of social life, ideology, mortality, political culture and a lack of religion have contributed to an alarming suicide rate. In comparison with other countries Hungary's suicide rate is twice that of the French, three and a half times that of the USA and five times that of the UK. Mortality from accidents and homicide (murder) are also significantly higher in Hungary, suggesting poor social integration and a poor feeling of belonging in this country.

This large-scale study suggests that we need to consider much wider factors than simply an individual's lifestyle if we are to understand factors affecting mortality and morbidity. These include social and economic factors, social class, race, education, sex, gender and even marital status (Hart, cited in Holland *et al.*, 1991).

EVALUATION OF HART'S (1991) STUDY

• This is a fascinating study that illustrates the power of social and economic factors in influencing our health.

- However, there may be other factors at work here (e.g. Tokyo may have a better infant and child care system than other countries) and these factors must also be considered.
- Although his arguments are persuasive, Hart does not adequately explain how the nature of these relationships operates in delivering such positive health outcomes or how they may impact on an individual's **quality of life**.

## Quality of life

Health psychology has increasingly recognised the need to focus on wider measures of health status than simply mortality and morbidity statistics. One of the measures that is gaining increasing acceptance is the quality of life measure. Quality of life is a conceptually difficult construct to define but the World Health Organisation Quality of Life (WHOQOL) Group in an attempt to consolidate previous definitions defined it as 'an individual's perception of their position in life in the context of culture and value systems in which they live and in relation to their goals, expectations, standards and concerns. It is a broad ranging concept affected in a complex way by a person's physical health, psychological state, level of independence, social relationships and their relationship to salient features in their environment'. As the definition states quality of life refers to an individual's *perceived* judgement about how satisfied they are with their life including health states and this may bear little resemblance to their actual physical health status.

For example, in one study involving patients undergoing treatment for **hypertension** (high blood pressure), patients rated their own quality of life following a treatment programme as much lower than their doctors did. Indeed, some patients and their families rated their quality of life to be lower than previous levels prior to receiving treatment (Jachuk *et al.*, 1982). This shows the subjective nature of quality of life and reinforces the need to ask patients themselves how they feel, rather than to simply infer how they must feel. More recently, however, health professionals have been used as judges in estimating Quality Adjusted Life Years (QALYs) for different disorders, providing a measure of the social worth of treatment, based on both immediate and future benefits to the patient (Skevington, 1995).

Recently the WHOQOL Group has been developing a cross-cultural quality of life instrument (the WHOQOL 100). This instrument has been used with many groups including patients who have chronic diseases (e.g. arthritis), those in high stress situations (e.g. migrants and refugees) and informal caregivers of the elderly and disabled (Skevington, 1995). It is a self-administered subjective assessment, has good psychometric properties, and covers a broad spectrum of the dimensions people have determined are important for quality of life.

Research suggests that there are not only individual differences in what constitutes quality of life but also cross-cultural differences in the weightings attached to these various factors as well. This makes measuring quality of life a challenging issue (Szabo *et al.* 1997).

Hyland and Kenyon (1992) have proposed a model of health-related quality-of-life constructs which includes a construct of *positive* evaluations (Hyland, 1992). The Satisfaction with Illness Scale (Hyland and Kenyon, 1992) was designed to assess positive ways in which illness has contributed to the patient's life, as indicated by the following statements:

1  Being ill has made me value my life more than I used to
2  I enjoy my life despite my problems
3  My illness has shown me the value of friendship
4  When I feel well, I feel really happy
5  My relatives really care about my problems
6  My illness has helped me learn about myself

Hyland and Kenyon (1992) studied 59 patients who were suffering from chronic obstructive pulmonary disease (a disease which involves breathlessness and substantial impairment of everyday activity). Using a seven-point scale, anchored by strongly agree and strongly disagree, he found that these items correlated with both patients' Satisfaction with Illness and Satisfaction with Life measures. This research suggests that illness may have positive quality of life consequences for patients. A comprehensive and readable review of quality of life theory and measurement can be found in Bowling (1997).

- Quality of life (QOL) is an extremely valuable construct for assessing how an individual feels about their health state and status.
- The subjective nature of quality of life, however, makes the reliability and cultural validity of the construct a challenging issue.
- Ethical issues involved in QOL ask whether it is possible to put a value on life, and what it means to do this. Afflicted individuals and their families might have a very different view from society about, for example, who should be kept alive on a respirator and for how long etc. There are also moral issues here (e.g. should life-sentence prisoners have equal chance of receiving life-saving surgery?).
- Hyland and Kenyon's (1992) research into quality of life suggests that illness may bring positive changes into a patient's life by making them learn more about themselves and appreciating their relatives and friends.

## Health policy

An understanding of epidemiology is not complete without some consideration of health policy. Health care, by definition, is an extremely valued and valuable resource and, in a population the size of the UK's (almost 60 million people in 1999), access to health resources has to be managed extremely carefully. The Labour Government's National Health Service Act of 1948 provided the foundation for the Minister of Health, Aneurin Bevan, to establish the National Health Service (NHS) which was to be available to all who required it and free at the point of delivery. Of course the reality is that the NHS is funded directly through taxation and indirectly through government block grants (i.e. it isn't free). Decisions about how best to allocate funds are made at national level by the Department of Health, and by Health Authorities and Health Service Providers.

In the UK, the medical profession has had a close relationship with the State, having both formal and informal rights to consultation on major policy changes. It has also operated with a great deal of clinical autonomy. With increasing emphasis now placed on efficiency in the Health Service, the power of the profession in both the political and medical spheres has been challenged. Health-care reforms have been brought in to change existing health-care practices and implement new ones. The UK is now moving towards a mixed economy of care where alternative ways of funding health-care include greater reliance on paying for care out of pocket or through medical insurance and also greater involvement of the voluntary sector. The importance of this is that access to health-care services is becoming an area of increasing concern and the need to reduce inequalities in health (e.g. rural, regional, etc.) will be one of the great health challenges of the new century.

The government's consultation paper *Our Healthier Nation: A Contract for Health* (1998) seeks to provide a 'middle way' between 'the old extremes of individual victim blaming on the one hand and nanny state social engineering on the other'. This middle way aims to be constructed by building and maintaining solid partnerships between individuals, families, local agencies and communities. The aim here is not only to be 'tough on the causes of ill-health' as the Minister for Public Health, Tessa Jowell, maintains, but also to address the causes of the causes: wider social and economic factors such as poverty, inequalities, social exclusion and unemployment (Milner, 1997).

In the international sphere, the UK has one of the lowest levels of total health-care expenditure as a percentage of gross domestic product (GDP: the total of a country's production of goods and services) of all the Organization for Economic Co-operation and Development (OECD) countries (see Table 2.1). The UK has spent, on average, less than 7 per cent of its GDP (the total value of goods and services produced) on total health-care expenditure between 1990 and 1997. In contrast, the USA spends twice as much with an average of almost 14 per cent on total health-care for the same period. Although direct comparisons in percentage terms of expenditure may not be valid, due to very different health-care systems, evidence shows that health-care policy is intimately linked with funding decisions. In turn, these decisions are taken and carried out on social, political and economic grounds.

## Summary

We have seen the work of epidemiologists in studying patterns of disease prevention and health promotion, focusing on the study of

*Table 2.1* Total health-care expenditure as per cent of GDP in selected OECD countries, 1990–1997

| | 1990 | 1991 | 1992 | 1993 | 1994 | 1995 | 1996 | 1997 |
|---|---|---|---|---|---|---|---|---|
| **OECD** | **7.1** | **7.4** | **7.6** | **7.7** | **7.7** | **7.7** | **7.7** | **7.7** |
| **EU15** | **7.4** | **7.7** | **7.9** | **8.0** | **7.9** | **7.9** | **8.0** | **7.9** |
| Australia | 8.3 | 8.6 | 8.6 | 8.5 | 8.5 | 8.4 | 8.5 | 8.3 |
| Canada | 9.2 | 9.9 | 10.3 | 10.2 | 9.9 | 9.7 | 9.6 | 9.3 |
| France | 8.9 | 9.1 | 9.4 | 9.8 | 9.7 | 9.9 | 9.7 | 9.9 |
| Germany | 8.7 | 9.4 | 9.9 | 10.0 | 10.0 | 10.4 | 10.5 | 10.4 |
| Greece | 4.2 | 4.2 | 4.5 | 5.0 | 5.4 | 5.8 | 6.8 | 7.1 |
| Italy | 8.1 | 8.4 | 8.5 | 8.6 | 8.4 | 7.7 | 7.8 | 7.6 |
| Japan | 6.0 | 6.0 | 6.4 | 6.6 | 7.0 | 7.2 | 7.2 | 7.3 |
| Spain | 6.9 | 7.0 | 7.3 | 7.5 | 7.4 | 7.3 | 7.4 | 7.4 |
| United Kingdom | 6.0 | 6.5 | 6.9 | 6.9 | 6.9 | 6.9 | 6.9 | 6.7 |
| United States | 12.6 | 13.4 | 13.9 | 14.1 | 14.1 | 14.1 | 14.0 | 14.0 |

*Source:* Adapted from Table 2.3 in *Compendium of Health Statistics*, 11th Edition, Office of Health Economics: London, 1999. Compiled by Peter Yeun.

populations. Changing patterns of health and illness over the last century have shown that the leading causes of death have changed dramatically, from fatal infectious diseases like tuberculosis to complex multi-factorial diseases such as heart disease and cancer. Insights into potential causes of diseases have allowed planning for effective prevention and treatment. Mortality and morbidity statistics have served as a useful tool in this process. Recently, quality of life has become a more appropriate method to use for policy making. It enables social and psychological factors to be considered and not just physical factors in assessing health states. Health policy issues are related to the above since health is now recognised as a valued resource, and access to health-care services is based on political, social and economic factors.

**Review exercise**

Imagine that you have been asked to make difficult funding decisions about how best to allocate a block grant for your local Health Authority. List ten groups of people who may need access to health-care services (e.g. diabetics, the mentally ill, etc.). What criteria might you employ about which groups take priority in terms of access to health-care services? With rationing of health-care resources now a reality in the UK, how best should we decide the fairest way to allocate health-care resources?

## Further reading

*Our Healthier Nation: A Contract for Health*, London: Stationery Office, 1998. This Labour Government Green Paper outlines government policy aimed at reducing inequalities in health and promoting healthy lifestyles, amongst a broad range of other health targets for the nation.

Pitts, M. and Phillips, K. (eds) (1998) *The Psychology of Health: An Introduction*, London: Routledge. Chapter 16 provides an excellent wide-ranging review of social circumstances, inequalities and health. It considers social class differences in health and illness together with gender, racial and ethnic differences in health. The new public health strategy, introduced by the Labour Government to combat the perceived causes of ill-health, is also reviewed.

Stroebe, W. and Stroebe, M. (1995) *Social Psychology and Health*, Buckingham: Open University Press. Chapter 1 provides a good overview of changing conceptions of health and illness over time and place and considers the relative roles of social and economic factors, psychological factors and lifestyles on health.

# 3

# Symptoms of illness and pain

Symptoms of illness and pain: adopting sick-role behaviour
Introduction to pain
Defining pain
History of pain
Characteristics of pain
Theories of pain
Summary

## Symptoms of illness and pain: adopting sick-role behaviour

How do people know when to seek medical attention? How do they know whether they are ill or sick? Deciding when oneself or others need medical attention is not always an easy decision, due in part to the problems of defining illness as discussed in Chapter 1. People may frequently experience physical symptoms which may or may not be related to an underlying illness. For example, persistent sniffles or sneezes would probably not prompt a person to seek medical care but severe stomach cramps probably would. According to Brannon and Feist (1997, p. 166), 'doctors not only determine illness by their diagnoses but also sanction it by giving a diagnosis'. It would appear that the doctor is the 'gatekeeper' to further health-care, including hospitalisation.

## Illness behaviour vs. sick-role behaviour

Kasl and Cobb (1966) distinguished between 'illness behaviour' and 'sick-role behaviour' in dealing with the symptoms of ill-health. **Illness behaviour** occurs *before* a diagnosis and consists of activities undertaken by people who experience symptoms of illness. These activities attempt to determine one's state of health and discover suitable remedies before visiting a doctor (e.g. taking paracetamol to relieve flu symptoms). '**Sick-role behaviour**', on the other hand, is the term applied to the behaviour of people following a diagnosis, usually from a doctor. These activities are aimed at getting well (e.g. keeping follow-up appointments, resting for a few days, etc.). It is therefore the diagnosis itself that separates illness behaviour from sick-role behaviour.

It is now known that a range of different factors influence when, where and how people look for help in their illness behaviour. These include:

- social and demographic factors
- symptom characteristics

## Social and demographic factors

There is reliable evidence of gender differences in use of health-care services, including visits to doctors. Women are, on average, twice as likely as men to visit their GP. This of course does not mean that women are less healthy than men are! On the contrary, women are known to be more sensitive to the symptoms they experience and this supports evidence that shows that women report more symptoms to their GP then men (Pennebaker, 1982). It is thought that these gender differences are due almost exclusively to social factors, with men reported to be at greater risk through alcohol problems and job hazards and women at greater risk through physical inactivity, non-employment and stress (Verbrugge, 1989). However, it could also be argued here that males are socialised into being 'strong' and so refuse to admit that their illness is serious enough to seek medical attention.

Socio-economic status (SES) factors also play a role here, with people in higher socio-economic groups experiencing fewer symptoms and reporting a higher level of health than people in lower socio-economic groups (Pennebaker, 1982). It is not clear, however, whether this relationship is correlational or causal. Interestingly, higher-SES people show higher levels of compliance in preventive health behaviours (especially cancer screening behaviour in women, for example, which shows a very steep SES–health gradient). However, when high-SES people are ill, they are more likely to seek health-care. People in low-SES groups tend to wait longer before receiving health-care, thus making treatment more difficult and hospitalisation more likely (Brannon and Feist, 1997).

There are also cultural and social factors involved in responding to symptoms of ill-health. Cultures differ in the degree to which they are socialised *not* to act with strong emotion when they are ill. Mechanic (1978) found that, in a review of studies of attitudes towards illness in different ethnic groups, Jewish Americans were more likely to seek professional help, accept the 'sick-role' and engage in preventive medical behaviours than Mexican Americans who tended to ignore symptoms that doctors considered serious and indeed inflated some symptoms that doctors considered as minor. Irish Americans were considered the most 'stoical' in denying pain, and these findings are similar to subsequent research by Clark and Clark (1980) on pain tolerance levels in Nepalese Sherpa soldiers, considered in the topic of pain below.

Finally, age is another demographic factor that influences symptom reporting and willingness to seek medical care. In general, young and middle-class adults show the greatest reluctance to seek health-care, with male adolescents showing the greatest reluctance (Garland and Zigler, 1994). If people attribute their symptoms to the ageing process, they tend to delay seeking medical care. Older adults are not as strongly influenced by this 'must be my age!' effect as middle-aged adults and seek medical advice sooner, even for similar complaints (Leventhal and Diefenbach, 1991). The authors explained this age effect in terms of the older patients' not wanting to tolerate uncertainty with their health and middle-aged adults wanting to minimise or even deny the severity of the illness.

### *Symptom characteristics*

In addition to the above social and demographic factors affecting reporting of symptoms, there is a need to look at the characteristics of the symptoms themselves, since these also affect how and when people seek help. People perceive and interpret their own symptoms in unique ways that are meaningful and often personal to them. They may, for example, use previous experience or their own lay-beliefs about how serious their symptoms are, and weigh up the rewards and costs of a visit to the doctor. Rewards might include symptom relief and reassurance. Costs might include interference with everyday life, time commitments and the possibility of receiving bad news.

Research by Mechanic (1978 cited in Brannon and Feist, 1997) listed four characteristics of the symptoms that determine an individual's response to illness:

### 1 Visibility of symptoms

This refers to how readily apparent (visible) the symptoms are, both to the individual and to other people. In general, individuals are more likely to seek help for visible symptoms than symptoms not expressed. Klohn and Rogers (1991) studied young women who were given messages about how to prevent **osteoporosis** (loss of bony tissue, resulting in brittle bones that are liable to fracture). Results showed that young women were much more likely to report intentions to adopt recommended precautions when alerted to possible disfiguring aspects of osteoporosis compared with young women who were not alerted to the disfiguring aspects. This study shows the importance of visibility of symptoms in influencing precautionary health behaviours.

### 2 Severity of symptoms

Mechanic (1978) predicted that the perceived seriousness of the symptoms would be related to seeking help (i.e. the more perceived seriousness of the symptom, the more likely this would be interpreted as requiring action). This was supported by Suchman (1965) who found that symptoms that were perceived as serious not only generated more concern in patients, but also were more likely to be interpreted as indicating illness. Indeed, Cameron *et al.* (1993) found that perceived severity of symptoms was considered more important than even the visible symptoms themselves (see 1 above) in the decision to seek health-care. Conversely, when people perceive the possibility of a major health problem, they may avoid going to the doctor for fear of discovering the worst. It is acknowledged that a person's own perception of severity may differ from that of a doctor or even hospital. Health professionals should therefore develop ways of ensuring that a patient's perception of their own symptoms are realistic and in accord with that of medical practitioners.

### 3 Interference of symptoms with daily living

Suchman (1965) found that the more incapacitated a person is, the more likely they were to seek medical care. This supports the view of Mechanic (1978) that symptoms were more likely to be interpreted as requiring medical help if they were considered to interfere with a person's life.

### 4 Frequency and persistence of symptoms

We tend to seek help from a doctor or other medical practitioner if we perceive our symptoms to be severe and continuous. A persistent pain is more likely than an intermittent one to result in an appointment being made to see a doctor. Prochaska *et al.* (1987) found that even mild symptoms resulted in individuals' seeking health-care from doctors (and friends and family) if their symptoms persisted.

In summary, research shows that all of these factors must be considered in predicting who seeks medical help and why. Mechanic (1978) states that symptoms alone are not necessarily sufficient for individuals to seek medical attention. Visibility, perceived seriousness, interference with daily living and persistence all play a role in seeking help and this occurs within a social context of family and friends.

## Social construction of health and illness

Similarly, an individual's personal views and knowledge of his or her own illness may lead to distortions in their thinking about causes, implications and treatments (e.g. Weinstein's (1984) notion of *unrealistic optimism* outlined earlier). Despite a vast amount of knowledge in medicine, biology, physiology and psychology, most people are largely ignorant of how their bodies work and how they become ill. Even well-educated people experience this problem, partly due to trying to incorporate explanations of health and illness into their existing knowledge structure. People's *conceptualisation of health and illness* therefore is a fascinating area in itself. For further research in this area, the reader is encouraged to read the excellent text, *Explaining Health and Illness* (Stainton-Rogers, 1991).

## Introduction to pain

**OUCH!** That hurts! Most of us will be able to relate to these expressions at various times in our lives when, for reasons perhaps not well noticed by us at the time, we engage in an action or behaviour that leads us to experience pain of varying intensity and duration. Indeed, in some cases, we may not even be aware of the pain until after the episode. In other cases, we may be aware of the pain but feel unable to control or reduce it. Psychologists have been interested in the study of pain since the realisation that it has a psychological dimension as well as a physical dimension.

According to Albert Schweitzer, 'pain is a more terrible lord of mankind than even death himself' (cited in Skevington, 1995, p. 1). Such a powerful indictment deserves further careful analysis of the nature of pain, what it means to those who experience it, and how best it can be managed or treated. This need is even more apparent when one considers that pain is the most common medical symptom presented to doctors when seeking help.

## Defining pain

Merskey *et al.* (1979) define pain as 'an unpleasant sensation or emotional experience which is associated with actual or potential tissue damage or is described in terms of such damage' (cited in Skevington, 1995, p. 8). This definition carries with it the notion that pain is *always* subjective and *always* unpleasant (hence an emotional experience). Merskey *et al.* further argue that experiences that resemble pain but are not unpleasant should not be labelled as pain and, likewise, unpleasant experiences without sensory qualities are not pain either. The role of psychological factors again becomes clear here since, subjectively, there is no way to distinguish between those who report pain due to tissue damage and those who experience pain without tissue damage. It seems sensible therefore not to tie the experience of pain to a particular stimulus (Skevington, 1995).

Decide which of the following events listed below would fit Merskey *et al.*'s (1979) definition of pain above. Try to justify why such events do or do not constitute a painful episode:

1 A person burns themselves whilst ironing, although withdrawing their hand quickly to avoid actual tissue damage.

2 A footballer is tackled from behind and writhes in apparent agony on the field, only to recover quickly when the referee fails to award their team a free-kick.

3 A patient is desolate following the death of a close relative.

4 A person is trapped in a lift and has a panic attack before being released.

*Progress exercise*

## History of pain

Ideas of pain and illness within Western cultures have changed significantly over the centuries. In the Middle Ages, military people viewed it with contempt and devalued it as womanly, while theologians saw it as a sign of divine correction (Duby, 1993 cited in Skevington, 1995). By the thirteenth century, Christ's suffering had become a central theme for all churchgoers, and it was only at this time that the idea emerged that pain was something that ought to be alleviated. Pain was considered as a necessary part of everyday life and was expected in a way not dissimilar to expectations of major epidemics such as influenza, pneumonia and tuberculosis (Taylor, 1995). In contrast, today, being in pain (a pain patient) means getting special attention. It is not seen as a biological condition but one that instead deserves care and concern.

The experience and meaning of pain appear to change across situations or cultures as well as over time. Cross-cultural studies show differences in *pain perception thresholds* (the lowest level of threshold necessary to detect pain 50 per cent of the time over a series of trials in which stimulus intensity of pain is increased). Studies also show even greater differences in reported *pain tolerance levels* or 'stoicism' (Skevington, 1995).

In a laboratory study, Clark and Clark (1980) found that Nepalese Sherpa porters needed higher intensities of electric shock than their

European employers did before they would describe them as painful! It would appear therefore that cultural factors give rise to social and developmental factors, and these influence the experience and reporting of pain. However, problems of small sample sizes, reliability of measures and participant expectations limit the degree of generalisability of these findings.

### An early model of pain

One of the earliest attempts to describe how pain operates was provided by Descartes's *Traité de l'homme* (1664) (cited in Melzack and Wall, 1965) and is illustrated in Figure 3.1. According to Descartes, the pain pathway extended from the base of the foot right up to the brain. Stepping on a fire would cause a reflex mechanism to operate in a manner similar to pulling a rope attached to a bell. The ringing of the bell would thus signify the pain experience! More sophisticated models are considered later in this chapter.

## Characteristics of pain

Although pain and injury appear to go hand in hand, the earlier definition of pain suggests that it may be possible to experience injury without pain, delayed pain following injury, pain without injury and pain out of proportion to the injury. All of these possible relationships

*Figure 3.1* Descartes's early model of pain

further add to the complexity and apparent paradoxes of this ubiquitous experience.

### 1 Injury without pain

Examples of injury without pain include congenital analgesia (a rare condition in which people are born with an inability to feel pain) and episodic analgesia (where people do feel pain although this experience is delayed by minutes or even hours after an injury). The tragic case of Miss C, a Canadian woman who had congenital analgesia, demonstrated the effects of being unable to experience pain. Miss C felt no pain when she was given electric shocks, or made contact with hot water or even when given an ice bath (all with her informed consent!). She did not show any of the expected physiological changes in response to these stimuli: her heart rate, respiration and blood pressure all remained stable. Miss C had problems with many of her joints, particularly her knees, hip and spine and died at the age of 29 when she developed massive infections that could not be controlled (Melzack and Wall, 1991 cited in Banyard, 1996). Remarkably, a post-mortem examination revealed no abnormalities of her nervous system, suggesting that **psychogenic** factors (rather than pathological) factors may be involved here. This study also suggests that the ability to experience pain is useful to our survival because it warns our bodies of possible danger.

Think of a recent occasion when you experienced physical pain. What was the first thing that you did? How did you react? Did the experience of pain focus your attention on the need to act quickly or did you try to 'tough it out'?

Progress exercise

### 2 Delayed pain following injury

A much more common form of analgesia occurs when we experience pain some time after an injury. A classic naturalistic observational study of injured soldiers rescued from Anzio beach during the Second World War appeared to demonstrate the role of psychological factors in mediating the pain experience. Beecher (1956, cited in Skevington, 1995) reported that only 25 per cent of injured soldiers requested an analgesic (pain relief). These soldiers were not in shock, were fully co-operative and were mentally clear. Soldiers who had sustained smaller wounds reported far more pain.

Beecher explained these findings in terms of the meaning of the pain experience in the context of war. Those soldiers with serious wounds interpreted their injuries as providing a 'ticket to safety' whilst those with minor wounds knew that they would be stitched up and sent back to the front line (Beecher, 1972 cited in Skevington, 1995). Social and environmental factors appeared to shape the experience of pain in this study. Similar findings have been reported by Carlen *et al.* (1978, cited in Melzack and Wall, 1991) who described the reaction of Israeli soldiers during the Yom Kippur War when they experienced traumatic amputations (having their limbs blown off). Many did not seem to be in a state of shock and were fully aware of the state of their injuries.

Such findings of episodic analgesia are not confined to war situations. Many sports injuries may result from an initial delay in the experience of pain, possibly due to social–psychological factors (e.g. intense competition). Melzack *et al.* (1982) studied 138 accident patients in the casualty department of a local hospital and asked them about their perceptions of pain. Significantly, 37 per cent reported not feeling any pain at the time of injury and that embarrassment appeared to be the most salient emotion! Although the majority reported that pain began within an hour of injury, in some cases the experience of pain was delayed by up to nine hours after their injury. In even more severe hospital cases, Bach *et al.* (1988 cited in Skevington, 1995) studied 25 amputees and found that, if given pre-operative pain relief (a lumbar epidural block within three days of surgery), none experienced pain even six months after surgery and the majority were still pain-free after one year.

## 3 Pain without injury

There are many examples of pain where there is no obvious physical cause, including neuralgia, **causalgia**, headache and **phantom limb** pain (Banyard, 1996). Neuralgia is a sudden sharp pain extending along a nerve pathway and may occur after a nerve-damaging disease (e.g. herpes) has ended. Causalgia is a burning pain that often develops as a consequence of a severe wound (e.g. a knife injury). Remarkably, both neuralgia and causalgia develop after the wound has healed and, although not constant pains, can be triggered by environmental stimuli (e.g. a stressful episode). Headaches (e.g. tension headaches, migraines) are surprisingly difficult to explain, particularly since early explanations in terms of particular muscle contractions do not adequately account for all types. Indeed, common explanations of migraine which refer to the dilation of blood vessels have been largely discounted since research suggests that changes in these blood vessels are more likely to be a result of headache than a cause (Melzack and Wall, 1991).

SUMMARY OF THE RELATIONSHIP BETWEEN INJURY AND PAIN

- These studies provide a useful insight into some of the charac-teristics associated with pain, although findings remain unclear because of problems of reliability in using self-report as a method of investigation and because of the atypical samples involved in these studies.
- It is often difficult to identify cause–effect relationships in study-ing injury and pain, not only because of the subjective nature of pain but also because injury and pain may relate in different ways to each other, depending on the event experienced.
- Injury may be difficult to detect in some cases (e.g. damage to a single neurone might lead to pain but would be virtually undetectable).

### 4 Phantom limb pain

**Phantom limb pain** has been of increasing interest to pain researchers as an alternative window into the pain experience. People who have lost a limb, or even those who were born without a limb, may experience all the sensations of having that limb and, remarkably, experience very real pain from their phantoms. Melzack (1992, cited in Banyard, 1996) reviewed the evidence on phantom limbs and found that phantom limb patients reported many common experiences. Phantom

**41**

limbs have a vivid sensory quality and can be located precisely in space by the individual. Patients may report a phantom arm as moving in co-ordination with other limbs when walking, even though in most cases it will hang down when the person is seated or standing. This is further enhanced when the individual is wearing an artificial arm or leg. Phantom limbs may experience a range of sensations, including pressure, warmth, cold, dampness and itching. Furthermore, more than two-thirds of all amputees suffer pain in the phantom. People with spinal injury may also experience phantoms. Paraplegics (people who have experienced paralysis of the lower limbs) may complain that their legs make continuous cycling movements producing painful fatigue, even though their actual legs are lying immobilised on the bed.

BIOLOGICAL EXPLANATION

Explanations for some of the above experiences may have a biological basis. Severed nerve ends may grow into nodules called 'neuromas' and these continue to produce nerve impulses that the brain interprets as coming from the lost limb. This explanation is difficult to test and has not received widespread support. In addition, the brain contains a network of **neurones** or neuromatrix that not only responds to sensory information but also itself generates a characteristic pattern of nerve impulses that indicate that the body is 'whole'. This is called a 'neuro-signature' (Melzack, 1992) and is considered to be largely pre-wired or innate. The neuromatrix continues to generate nerve impulses from the lost limb, even in the absence of sense data. Interestingly Melzack also believes that this neuromatrix has nervous system pathways from the emotional and motivational systems and from pathways associated with the recognition of self, suggesting the exciting potential for psychological interventions and treatments.

## 5 Pain out of proportion to the injury

It is also interesting to note that the amount of pain reported or experienced does not always match the amount of injury. Some cancers, for example, may cause massive injury to the body but produce very little pain until they are very advanced, whilst comparatively minor complaints that produce very little damage or threat (e.g. kidney stones passing to the ureter) can produce excruciating pain (Banyard, 1996). Again, pain appears to be an intensely personal and subjective experience and this may or may not relate to physical or pathological factors.

## Theories of pain

Theories of pain have advanced significantly since Descartes's *Traité de l'homme* (1664) model, mentioned above. Although beautiful in its simplicity and elegance, Descartes was writing at a time when there was no knowledge of neurophysiological processes. Indeed it was not until 1842 that sophisticated methodology allowed researchers to understand that pain is carried to the brain by pain nerves.

### Specificity theory

This theory built on Descartes's model by proposing a special system of nerves (or **nociceptors**) which carry messages from pain receptors in the skin to a pain centre in the brain. Specificity theories believe that there is a one-to-one relationship between a neural structure and our psychological experience of pain. Recent research using neurography (recording the activity of specific nerves and matching this up with reported sensations) shows that this relationship is over-simplified.

A related problem with this approach is that it assumes that fibres would produce pain alone and not other sensations. We now know that there are different types of neurones involved in pain discrimination. These involve large, heavily **myelinated** (fast-conducting) **A-beta fibres (cutaneous)**, more thinly myelinated (slower) **A-delta fibres (cutaneous)** and finer, unmyelinated **C fibres**. Each of these fibres responds to different features of the pain experience and in different ways (e.g. excitation or inhibition of spinal cord cells) as a result of different types of stimulation (Skevington, 1995). For example, we have pain receptors that detect heat and other receptors that detect touch.

### Pattern theories

These theories go against specificity theory by suggesting that there are no separate systems for perceiving pain. Instead, nerves are shared with other senses such as touch. Furthermore, pain fibres ascend and descend to and from the brain and we now know that some form of spatial summation (adding together pain sensations from different senses or the same sense on different occasions) and analysis also occurs in this cycle. The exact areas involved, and the nature of this process, remain unclear. Recent research suggests that this summation acts across different segments of the spinal cord and operates across the range of the pain experience, from early detection to maximum tolerance (Nielson and Arendt-Nielson, 1997). The best-known example of pattern theory is the gate control theory.

### Gate control theory

The gate control theory was first proposed by Melzack and Wall in 1965 in a now famous paper, 'Pain mechanisms: a new theory', published in the journal *Science*. This theory combined the medical approach of the previous theories with the more recent biopsychosocial model of health (Engel, 1977). This approach considers the interaction of biological, psychological and social factors in pain

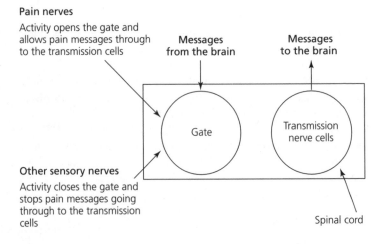

**Figure 3.2 Gate control theory**
*Source*: Curtis (1999), adapted from Banyard (1996).

and not simply the medical factors alone. The gate control theory is illustrated in Figure 3.2.

This model is biologically complex to understand and the description of the nervous system pathways involved is beyond the scope of this text. The theory suggests that there is a 'gate' or, more precisely, a gating mechanism in the nervous system. This opens and closes in response to various factors. Opening the gate allows pain messages to travel to the brain. Closing the gate stops messages travelling to the brain.

Activity in the pain fibres cause **transmission cells (T-cells)** to send pain signals to the brain and open the gate. Activity in sensory nerves not directly linked to pain causes larger-diameter nerves to carry information about 'harmless' sensations (e.g. touching, rubbing or scratching). These activities close the gate and reduce the likelihood of the pain experience. That is why rubbing an injured leg can alleviate the pain. Messages from the brain itself can also close or open the gate. Excitement or anxiety can have different effects on the gating mechanism and distracting someone in pain may actually involve closing their gate! This model suggests that pain is a two-way flow of information to and from the brain and that the brain not only processes this information but also directly affects the

Use Table 3.1 to suggest how the operation of different factors may open (pain) or close (no pain) the gate. One example is given for you for each category. Try to think of one more for each category.

*Table 3.1* **Factors affecting the gating mechanism**

|  | Conditions that open the Gate | Conditions that close the Gate |
| --- | --- | --- |
| Physical | Extent of injury/ tissue damage | Massage |
| Emotional | Anxiety | Relaxation |
| Mental | Focusing on the pain | Distraction from the pain |

Review exercise

gating mechanism. The nature of how the gating mechanism works, however, remains unclear and further research is required in this area.

EVALUATION OF GATE CONTROL THEORY

- This model has received much empirical support from a range of studies, although the exact mechanisms involved in the pain process are still not known.
- There remains no direct evidence of either the gating mechanism or the transmission cells (T-cells) although it is assumed that these exist in some form in the nervous system.
- The model is the best available for explaining many of the above puzzling characteristics of pain by recognising the need to include psychological factors (e.g. cognition, emotion) and not simply physical factors in understanding pain.

## Summary

We have explored here the nature and characteristics of pain and considered the relationship between pain and injury. Models of pain have become more sophisticated as our understanding of the pain experience has developed and there is increasing recognition of the role of psychological factors in pain. Specificity theories assume a one-to-one relationship between a neural structure and our psychological experience of pain. Pattern theories build on this idea although they suggest that nerves involved in pain are shared with other senses. Further, spatial summation suggests that the pain experience is the product of summing different sensations in the spinal cord. An example of this, the gate control theory, remains one of the most plausible and exciting models of pain both for further understanding of the mechanisms involved and the implications for designing effective treatments.

## Further reading

Melzack, R. and Wall, P. D. (1991) *The Challenge of Pain*, rev. edn, London: Penguin. This original pain textbook provides a very readable account of the puzzle of pain. It emphasises the need to consider psychological factors in addition to physiological factors

in understanding the pain experience and this is further emphasised in a very comprehensive discussion of the gate control theory
of pain, which the authors originated.

Ogden, J. (1996) *Health Psychology: A Textbook*, Buckingham: Open
University Press. Chapter 11 reviews the early models of pain and
considers the gate control theory of pain in contrast to these earlier
models. The role of psychosocial factors in pain perception is also
explored together with the contribution that psychology can make
in the treatment of pain.

Pitts, M. and Phillips, K. (eds) (1998) *The Psychology of Health: An
Introduction*, 2nd edn, London: Routledge. This excellent text
provides a comprehensive chapter on the main theories of pain
and considers psychological aspects of pain. The assessment,
treatment and management of pain are also considered.

Skevington, S. M. (1995) *The Psychology of Pain*, Chichester: Wiley.
This text provides a comprehensive, integrated and accessible
account of the experience of pain and considers implications for
the management and treatment of pain and for **coping** processes.

# 4

# Pain: assessment, management and treatment

Measuring pain
Medical treatments for pain
Psychological treatments of pain
Multimodal approaches
Multidisciplinary treatments: the pain clinic
Summary

### Measuring pain

The measurement of pain is a difficult issue, due in part to the subjective nature of the pain experience discussed earlier. It is important to be able to measure and assess pain, however, so that it can be controlled and managed. For example, in deciding whether a particular intervention has been successful in reducing pain, pre- and post-treatment measures are usually compared. The following techniques have been used to measure pain (see Brannon and Feist, 1997 for a more extensive review).

#### *Physiological measures*

Pain usually produces an emotional response and, because the role of the autonomic nervous system (ANS) is known to be implicated in strong emotional arousal (see later chapters on stress here), it could be assumed that physiological measures may provide a measure of pain.

However, the research evidence is mixed here. Syrjala and Chapman (1984 cited in Brannon and Feist, 1997) have identified the following three physiological variables as potential measures of pain.

### 1 Muscle tension

Electromyography (EMG) has been used to measure the level of muscle tension in patients suffering from low back-pain. Results show that EMG recordings can reveal abnormal patterns of muscle activity, although these results do not consistently correlate with reported severity of the pain (Wolf *et al.*, 1982). Similarly, Andrasik *et al.* (1982) used a variety of physiological measures, including forehead and forearm EMGs, but found no support for the notion that muscle tension is a valid predictor of recurrent headaches. These studies, and others, suggest that muscle tension, as measured by electromyography, is not a reliable or valid measure of pain and that there is a need to consider other factors here.

### 2 Autonomic ('self-regulating') indices

Autonomic indices involve the measurement of involuntary processes such as hyperventilation, blood flow in the temporal artery (supplying blood to the temple and scalp), heart rate, hand surface temperature, finger pulse volume and skin resistance level. As above, these measures have only limited success in measuring pain. For example, Glynn *et al.* (1981) found that chronic pain patients showed more hyperventilation (uncontrolled rapid and deep respiration) than a control group who were no longer suffering from pain.

### 3 Evoked potentials

Evoked potentials are electrical signals generated by the brain in response to sensory stimuli. They are similar in nature to **electro-encephalograms (EEGs)** which measure the entire electrical activity of the brain, although evoked potentials focus instead on areas of the brain that receive input from the various senses (e.g. visual, auditory). The problem here is that evoked potentials are not specific enough to measure pain and only pain. However, a review of research on evoked potentials by Syrjala and Chapman (1984 cited in Brannon and Feist

1997) concluded that this technique has *some* capacity to distinguish the responses of patients with chronic pain and responses of people in a control group who did not suffer pain. However, the same researchers also found that evoked potentials may increase even when subjective reports of pain remain constant, suggesting that this physiological measure also lacks reliability and validity.

### Behavioural assessment

An obvious possible answer to the question of how best to measure pain is to simply observe and record the pain patient's behaviour! People who are in pain often grimace, limp, sigh, rub, miss work or remain in bed and are absent from work. They engage in behaviours that signify to observers that they may be suffering from pain (Fordyce, 1976). Fordyce suggests that each of these behaviours has potential reward value that reinforces such behaviours (e.g. attention, sympathy, compensation) and, in being reinforced, makes them more likely to be repeated again. This is one of the basic tenets of behaviourist theory and explains how **operant conditioning** works.

Fordyce (1976) and other researchers have subsequently trained spouses and others close to the pain patient to make careful observations of the pain behaviour without reinforcing it. This has also been accompanied with the use of a 'spouse-diary' and a 'significant pain questionnaire' (Turk *et al.*, 1983). Although this technique can be considered high on ecological validity (i.e. 'real-life' validity), it is limited in terms of the amount of control significant others may have in measuring the pain experience. Increases in reliability have been found when these techniques are extended to pain clinics (see previous chapter) and laboratory settings using trained observers.

### Self-reports

*1 Rating scales*

Self-reports include sample rating scales, psychometrically standardised pain inventories and personality tests. One of the simplest rating scales asks patients to rate their intensity of pain on a scale from 1 to 100 with 100 being the most excruciating pain possible and 1 being the least amount of pain detectable, as shown in Figure 4.1.

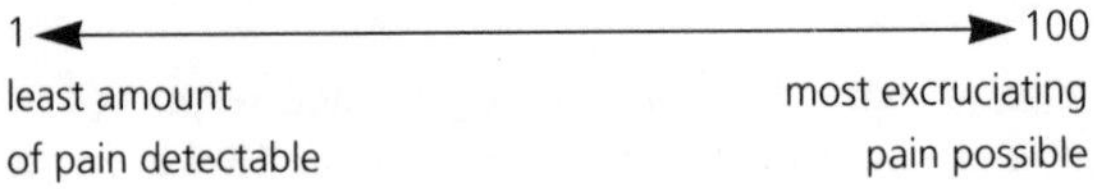

1 ◄─────────────────────────────► 100

least amount                              most excruciating
of pain detectable                         pain possible

*Figure 4.1* **Pain intensity scale**

A similar technique uses the visual analogue scale (VAS) which simply involves anchoring a line on the left with a phrase like 'no pain' and on the right by a phrase like 'worst pain imaginable'. The patient merely places a mark somewhere on this scale to indicate the intensity of their pain. Because the scale has no exact marked units, it is considered to be a more sensitive measure, allowing effective comparisons to be made. Both the numerical scale and the VAS have been shown to have acceptable reliability ratings (Kremer *et al.*, 1981) although they have been criticised as being confusing to older patients and not considering the many different dimensions of pain.

*2 Pain questionnaires*

Melzack (1975) was highly critical of the above rating scales, arguing that measuring pain in this way was like specifying our visual world only in terms of light, without considering its pattern, colour or texture. He therefore developed the McGill Pain Questionnaire (MPQ) in 1975. The MPQ provides a subjective measure of pain and categorises pain under three dimensions:

- Sensory Qualities (this refers to the temporal, spatial, pressure and thermal properties of pain). This is similar to identifying the *physical* dimensions of pain.
- Affective Qualities (this refers to the fear, tension and autonomic qualities of pain). This is similar to identifying the *feelings* associated with the pain.
- Evaluative Qualities (this refers to the subjective overall intensity of the pain experience). This is similar to identifying the *meaning* of the pain experience.

The MPQ has four parts: Part 1 consists of front and back drawings of a human body in which patients mark where they feel their pain (see Figure 4.2). Part 2 consists of 20 sets of words describing pain.

Patients have to draw a circle around the *one* word in *each* set that most accurately describes their pain, as shown in Figure 4.3. Note that the adjectives here are ordered from least to most painful within each category to give some measure of intensity of the pain experience. Part 3 asks patients how their pain has changed over time, to give some measure of the persistency of pain, and Part 4 measures the intensity of pain using a five-point scale, ranging from mild to excruciating pain. This yields a Present Pain Intensity (PPI) score which, encouragingly, correlates well with the visual analogue scale (VAS) described earlier.

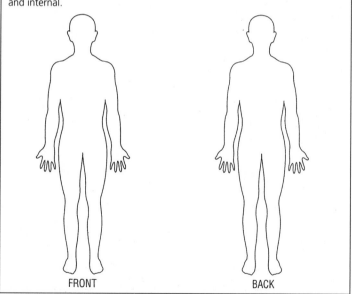

**Part 1. Where is your pain?**

Please mark, on the drawing below, the areas where you feel pain. Put E if external, or I if internal, near the areas which you mark. Put EI if both external and internal.

FRONT          BACK

*Figure 4.2* **Extract from MPQ Pain Measure**

*Source:* Part 1 of figure originally titled 'Extract from McGill Pain Questionnaire'. Reprinted from *Pain*, 1, R. Melzack, 'The McGill Pain Questionnaire: Major properties and scoring methods', 277–99, Copyright 1975, with permission from Elsevier Science.

Some of the words below describe your *present* pain. Circle *ONLY* those words that best describe it. Leave out any category that is not suitable. Use only a single word in each appropriate category – the one that applies best.

| 1 | 2 | 3 | 4 |
|---|---|---|---|
| Flickering | Jumping | Pricking | Sharp |
| Quivering | Flashing | Boring | Cutting |
| Pulsing | Shooting | Drilling | Lacerating |
| Throbbing | | Stabbing | |
| Beating | | Lancinating | |
| Pounding | | | |

| 5 | 6 | 7 | 8 |
|---|---|---|---|
| Pinching | Tugging | Hot | Tingling |
| Pressing | Pulling | Burning | Itchy |
| Gnawing | Wrenching | Scalding | Smarting |
| Cramping | | Searing | Stinging |
| Crushing | | | |

| 9 | 10 | 11 | 12 |
|---|---|---|---|
| Dull | Tender | Tiring | Sickening |
| Sore | Taut | Exhausting | Suffocating |
| Hurting | Rasping | | |
| Aching | Splitting | | |
| Heavy | | | |

| 13 | 14 | 15 | 16 |
|---|---|---|---|
| Fearful | Punishing | Wretched | Annoying |
| Frightful | Gruelling | Blinding | Troublesome |
| Terrifying | Cruel | | Miserable |
| | Vicious | | Intense |
| | Killing | | Unbearable |

| 17 | 18 | 19 | 20 |
|---|---|---|---|
| Spreading | Tight | Cool | Nagging |
| Radiating | Numb | Cold | Nauseating |
| Penetrating | Drawing | Freezing | Agonizing |
| Piercing | Squeezing | | Dreadful |
| | Tearing | | Torturing |

*Figure 4.3* **Pain adjectives used in the MPQ**

*Source:* Part 2 of figure originally titled 'Extract from McGill Pain Questionnaire'. Reprinted from *Pain*, 1, R. Melzack, 'The McGill Pain Questionnaire: Major properties and scoring methods', 277–99, Copyright 1975, with permission from Elsevier Science.

- The MPQ is the most widely and frequently used multi-dimensional measure of pain and has been used to assess pain relief in a variety of treatment programmes.
- In terms of its validity (i.e. measuring what it claims to measure), it has demonstrated moderate validity in assessing cancer pain, headaches and several other pain syndromes (Brannon and Feist, 1997)
- The MPQ has, however, been criticised in terms of its difficult vocabulary and for not having a standard scoring format. Although useful in describing the quality of the pain experience, the MPQ may produce both oral and written responses that may not necessarily be equivalent.

Other pain questionnaires include a short form of the McGill (SF-MFQ), developed by Melzack in 1987 with fewer decriptors but strong correlations with the original McGill questionnaire, indicating good alternative form reliability (i.e. consistent agreement using a different instrument).

## Medical treatments for pain

For centuries, doctors and other health practitioners have used a variety of means for alleviating pain. Using the medical model, treatments were initially physical in nature (e.g. drugs) but it is now recognised that the most effective treatments are those that are supplemented with psychological and behavioural techniques. This supports the view expressed in the last chapter that, since pain is subjective in nature and mediated by psychological factors, then treatment should reflect such a person-centred and eclectic approach (i.e. not following any one particular theoretical position).

### Medical treatments

Medical treatments for pain have varied according to the nature and location of the pain experience. For example, acute pain (sudden onset) is usually treated with drugs although acute and chronic (gradual onset, long-lasting) pain have been treated by stimulation to the skin, using either electrical impulses (transcutaneous electrical neural stimulation or TENS) or needles (**acupuncture**). If chronic pain does not respond to any of these treatments, then surgery may be considered.

## 1 Drugs

Analgesic drugs relieve pain without causing loss of consciousness and are usually one of two main types:

- Aspirin type: this uses an active component called 'salicin' which, as well as having analgesic (pain-relieving) properties, also helps prevent inflammation and fever. For this reason, they are also called 'non-steroidal anti-inflammatory drugs' (or NSAIDs). These drugs are particularly useful for pain in which injury has occurred.
- Opium type: the extract of the opium poppy has been used for at least 5,000 years, with its analgesic properties being known to the ancient Romans, although morphine was only isolated from this compound in 1803. These drugs are very powerful and produce pain relief in a very similar way to several neurotransmitter substances in the brain. Many doctors are reluctant to prescribe morphine in amounts strong enough to reduce intense pain. This is because the drug is so powerful.

Recent research has focused on the use of drugs that modify the neurotransmitter function of monoamines (e.g. **serotonin**, **noradrenaline** and **dopamine**). These drugs are now known to modify the sensitivity of pain in response to noxious stimuli in mammalian species, including humans (Budd, 1994). One challenge now is to incorporate such pharmacological insights into the gate control theory of pain (see previous chapter).

## 2 Transcutaneous electrical neural stimulation (TENS)

TENS treatment has been successfully used since the early 1970s, most notably with arthritis patients and for childbirth pain relief. Electrodes are placed on the surface of the skin (covering about 4 cm of the skin surface) and are then electrically stimulated. Many of these units are portable and run on re-chargeable batteries. Patients can control the strength and duration of stimulation to suit their needs. Results show that pain relief is not only achieved during stimulation but also persists for hours after stimulation has ceased. This technique has been used effectively to treat both acute and chronic pain.

EVALUATION OF TENS

- The use of TENS has not been reliably demonstrated to be more effective as an analgesic in pain relief compared with drug therapy or surgery, although TENS patients did request fewer doses of drugs to control their pain and were discharged sooner from hospital compared with standard post-surgery care (Nelson and Planchock, 1989).
- Comparison of TENS with **placebo** control trials (in which patients are led to believe that they were receiving pain relief but in fact there was no active agent) showed no significant differences in pain relief for pregnant women during the first stage of labour (van der Ploeg *et al.*, 1996). This suggests that there may be a placebo effect involved (e.g. expectation of relief may have contributed to observed effects).
- However, a review of the use of TENS with arthritis patients by Melzack and Wall (1982) showed that TENS produced significant pain relief. It was also considered to be effective for patients who had not received relief following other treatment methods, including surgery.

*3 Acupuncture*

Acupuncture is an ancient Chinese form of analgesia that consists of inserting needles into specific points on the skin and then continuously stimulating them, either electrically or by manually twirling the needles. This technique has not been widely accepted by all Western medical practitioners (in contrast to China, for example, where it is used as a sole means of analgesia in some types of surgery!). Indeed, even in countries where the technique is well developed, only about 10 per cent of all patients experience sufficient analgesia during surgery to relieve pain. Furthermore, the effects of analgesia are not immediate. The needles must be stimulated for about 20 minutes to produce analgesia and the stimulation must be fairly intense and continuous.

- Although acupuncture takes time to produce analgesic effects, once produced the analgesic effect can last for many hours after the stimulation has ceased.
- Melzack and Wall (1982) found acupuncture to be more effective than a placebo in producing pain relief and, since it can produce analgesia in both dogs and monkeys, cannot be explained by the placebo (or expectancy) effect alone. Again, the exact mechanisms through which this technique operates remain unclear.
- Chapman and Gunn (1990) maintain, after ten years of research into this field, that no firm conclusions can be drawn on the effectiveness of acupuncture and, although considered quite safe as an alternative to traditional techniques, its use as a treatment for pain relief remains experimental.

## 4 Surgery

The use of surgery in treating pain is the most extreme method and, therefore, only tends to be used as a last resort and when other techniques have failed. In particular, it has been used to alleviate the symptoms of low back pain. Of course, not all patients experience analgesia from surgery (as with other techniques), and surgery may result in additional complications and dangers if it is unsuccessful.

Surgery to control pain can occur at any level of the nervous system. Possible sites for surgery include the peripheral nerves close to the site of the pain. This is particularly advised if the pain is localised. Even then, the localisation should allow only limited destruction of pain nerves and there should be good knowledge that destruction will result in pain relief. A local anaesthetic is used first here, so that the patient can still report sensations at different sites. Some patients would rather suffer the pain than the complete loss of sensation that such surgery may involve. Another potential problem here is that, in most cases, the peripheral nerves include both sensory and motor fibres. Damage or destruction could result in loss of movement as well as loss of sensation, a price most definitely not worth paying by the majority of pain sufferers. Nerves in this peripheral section regenerate (unlike nerves in the cental nervous system) so the entire nerve section needs to be destroyed if the pain is not to return when the nerves regenerate.

Surgery in the dorsal root ganglion (just outside the spinal cord) involves severing sensory loss only, not motor loss (nerves split into dorsal and ventral branches before entering the spinal cord). Such patients thus lose sensation but retain movement, although Carson (1987) reports that, such is the distress at losing sensation, some patients may develop 'phantom-limb'-type experiences after surgery (see previous chapter).

Other sites for surgical intervention involve the spinal cord (in particular the spinothalamic tract) and the brain itself. In the case of the former, there is usually a complete loss of sensation for the area of the body below the damage. Hence this form of surgery is usually only performed on patients with terminal conditions who would benefit from pain relief for the remainder of their lives (Brannon and Feist, 1997). Brain surgery to relieve pain is both rare and obviously very serious, since lesions to the brain produce many effects in addition to pain relief. Pre-frontal lobotomies produce pain relief (in terms of decreased concern with pain) with no apparent sensory deficits. Patients appear to have such little concern with the resultant sensation that they do not report pain. Surgery to the thalamus and the somatosensory cortex are both dangerous and not proven to be effective in pain relief. On a more promising note, the implantation of devices that stimulate the brain to produce pain relief (e.g. using a small electrode in the periaqueductal grey of the brain) has been shown to help control pain (Carson, 1987). Similarly, introducing an opiate drug directly into the ventricles of the brain has also yielded pain relief; the drug spreads throughout the brain, operating on the opiate receptors, and relieving pain by a more direct route than oral, intramuscular or intravenous routes.

## Psychological treatments of pain

The previous chapter showed how psychological factors play a significant role in the experience of pain. Consistent with this view, treatments have also considered the role that psychology may play in alleviating pain symptoms. These treatment methods include hypnosis, relaxation training, **biofeedback**, behaviour modification, cognitive therapy (including self-efficacy), and multi-modal approaches (see Brannon and Feist, 1997 for a more extensive review).

## 1 Hypnosis

The use of hypnosis to alleviate pain remains a controversial issue. Indeed, even the nature of hypnosis, and the mechanisms through which it operates, are strongly debated issues. Hilgard (1979) regards hypnosis as an altered *state* of consciousness in which the person's stream of consciousness is divided or dissociated. Alternatively, Barber (1984) argues that hypnosis is more like a generalised *trait* that is a relatively stable characteristic of an individual.

According to Hilgard, the process of *induction* (being placed in a hypnotic state) allows an individual to respond to suggestion and to control physiological processes that would be impossible in the normal state of consciousness. Barber disagrees with this notion, arguing that suggestibility is effective in the absence of a trance-like state. Both researchers agree, however, that hypnosis is a highly effective clinical tool that may help in the control of pain, although both also recognise that those who are more suggestible to hypnosis will derive greater benefit. Evidence suggests that hypnosis is only effective for certain types of pain, including childbirth, headache, cancer pain, low back pain, myofascial pain and laboratory-induced pain, although Brannon and Feist (1997) maintain that the important variable here is the type of patient not the type of pain.

The main controversy here is whether hypnosis works by actually '*blocking out*' the experience of pain in some way or whether it merely lowers the *reporting* of pain (as we saw earlier, the reporting of pain may be influenced by social and cultural factors). Hilgard's (1979) notion of dissociated consciousness allows for the possibility that hypnotised people given a *suggestion* of analgesia will still experience the physical sensations of pain, but if the hypnotist has suggested that they will not feel pain, then they may report that they do not. Interestingly, Hilgard and Hilgard (1975) found that highly hypnotisable patients, given the suggestion that they feel no pain, still rated their pain as substantial when told to report all sensations under hypnosis, even though they showed few behavioural signs of pain and verbalised little or no discomfort.

PAIN: ASSESSMENT, MANAGEMENT AND TREATMENT

In contrast to the suggestibility hypothesis, Orne (1980) found that under hypnosis people still show behavioural signs of pain and that important physiological changes in respiration, heart rate and blood pressure *still* accompany increases in pain. This suggests that the individual is experiencing pain but is able to block it out. It would appear therefore that hypnosis operates on the subjective reporting elements of pain and not on the underlying physiological mechanisms.

- Whatever the nature of the effects, there is little doubt that hypnosis helps in pain relief. Van der Does and Van Dyck (1989) reviewed 28 studies that used hypnosis with burns patients and found consistent evidence that hypnosis is an effective analgesia for alleviating burn pain (i.e. people said that they did not feel pain).
- There was no evidence, however, that hypnosis could speed up the healing process. Hypnosis appears to be most successful in blocking the experience of pain.
- It appears that hypnosis can and does provide pain relief (analgesia) for certain types of people (who are susceptible) and for certain types of pain although the precise mechanisms for relief remain unclear.

*2 Relaxation training*

This technique dates back as far as hypnosis and is possibly the simplest technique to use for treating pain. Although used by the ancient Egyptians, Hebrews and Tibetans as a form of healing through rhythmic breathing and chanting, the modern psychological equivalent to relaxation training is credited to Jacobson's (1934, 1938) progressive relaxation technique. In progressive muscle relaxation, people learn to relax one muscle group at a time, progressing through the entire range of the body's muscle groups, until the whole body is relaxed. There are different relaxation techniques designed for treating a range of conditions including hypertension, tension headaches, chronic pain, burn pain, nausea and anxiety (e.g. following chemotherapy).

### 3 Progressive muscle relaxation

With progressive muscle relaxation training, patients are first explained the rationale for the procedure, including an explanation that their present tension is mostly a physical state resulting from tense muscles. Reclined in a comfortable chair with no distracting lights or sounds, patients first breathe deeply and then exhale slowly. Following this, deep muscle relaxation begins in which patients are instructed to first tense a selected muscle group (e.g. the foot) and hold the resultant tension for about 10 seconds. Slowly, they are asked to release this tension, focusing on the relaxation, as the tension gradually fades away. The sequence is then repeated, focused on a different muscle group and so on, working up the body from the toes, feet, calves and thighs to the shoulders, neck, mouth, tongue and forehead. Patients repeat the breathing exercise until they are deeply relaxed. During this experience, patients are often encouraged to focus on the pleasant feeling of relaxation, rating it on a scale of 1 to 10, or signalling with an index finger when tension begins to increase. Once established, this technique can be practised at home with the option of using soothing audio cassettes of their instructor's voice! The length of relaxation training sessions varies, although ten sessions over 6–8 weeks usually teaches deep relaxation to patients.

### 4 Meditative relaxation

Meditative relaxation derives from various religious meditative practices although, as used by psychologists, it has no religious connotations in treatment. Developed by Benson (1974), it combines muscle relaxation with a quiet environment, comfortable position, a repetitive sound, and a passive attitude. Participants sit with their eyes closed and muscles relaxed (see above). They then focus on their breathing and repeat silently a sound (e.g. 'one' or 'om') with each breath for about 20 minutes. This prevents distracting thoughts and maintains muscle relaxation.

### 5 Mindfulness meditation

This is an alternative to meditative relaxation and, with its roots in Buddhism, has been used to successfully treat people suffering from stress, anxiety or pain. In this treatment, people do not try to ignore unpleasant thoughts or sensations by focusing on their breathing or a single sound but rather focus on and embrace these thoughts as they occur. As these thoughts enter consciousness, they are asked to observe them in a non-judgemental way and this allows the individual to gain self-insight into how they see the world and what motivates them. This objective stance of 'pure fleeting thoughts and images' is believed to provide a window into our mind's consciousness, helping us to relax through self-discovery.

*6  Guided imagery*

This technique is similar to meditative relaxation in procedure, except that here patients are encouraged to conjure up a calm, peaceful image (e.g. the rhythmic roar of a blue ocean or a beautiful still area of English countryside in summer-time!). They then focus on a painful or anxious situation, whilst still retaining the image of peace and beauty. Guided imagery assumes that a person cannot concentrate on more than one image at once – the pleasant scene is so delightful or powerful that it averts attention away from the painful experience. Variations of guided imagery focus on imagining extremely *unpleasant* situations to block intense feelings of pain, relying on intensity rather than pleasantness. This may also involve real-life situations, a procedure called 'in-vivo' imagery.

EFFECTIVENESS OF RELAXATION TRAINING

In a review of different studies, Brannon and Feist (1997) investigated the effectiveness of different relaxation techniques for different kinds of problems. This is illustrated in Table 4.1.

The review suggests that relaxation training is effective for treating hypertension although it should complement drug therapy rather than replace it. It is, however, particularly effective in the treatment of chronic pain, although many of these studies lacked suitable control groups. Meditation has been shown to be effective in reducing stress, anxiety, phobias and hypertension, and mindfulness meditation was demonstrated to be more effective in the treatment of chronic pain than traditional methods, including the use of analgesics (Kabat-Zinn *et al.*, 1985). Guided imagery was found to be of similar effectiveness

### Table 4.1 Effectiveness of relaxation techniques

| Problem | Relaxation technique | Effectiveness |
| --- | --- | --- |
| Hypertension | Several types of relaxation training | Effective for mild hypertension<br>Not as effective as drugs |
| Tension headache | Progressive relaxation | More effective than placebo<br>As effective as biofeedback |
| Anxiety | Meditative relaxation | As effective as relaxation training |
| Chronic pain | Mindfulness meditation | Better than physical therapy or medication |
| Anxiety | Mindfulness meditation | Effective for 90 per cent of people |
| Nausea and anxiety from chemotherapy | Guided imagery plus progressive relaxation | More effective than no treatment |
| Burn pain | Guided imagery plus relaxation | More effective than other combinations of relaxation therapy |

*Source*: From *Health Psychology: An Introduction to Behavior and Health, 3/e, 3rd edition* by L. Brannon and J. Feist. © 1997. Reprinted with permission of Wadsworth Publishing, a division of International Thomson Publishing. Fax 800 730-2215.

to meditation and progressive relaxation in pain management and most studies show further benefits when these treatments are carefully integrated and used in combination treatments.

*7 Biofeedback*

Most people in the Western world assumed that it is not possible to consciously control physiological processes such as heart rate, the secretion of digestive juices and the constriction of blood vessels.

Such biological functions do not require *conscious* attention for their regulation and attempts to consciously control autonomic nervous system function met with little success. Then in the late 1960s and with increasingly sophisticated technology, a number of researchers found that biofeedback may indeed be possible in selected areas, and for selected processes. Biofeedback allows immediate feedback to individuals about the status of their biological systems. Individuals learn, for example, to increase and decrease their heart rate in response to feedback and even control visceral responses (e.g. salivation, intestinal contractions and blood pressure) with sufficient training (Miller, 1969). Today, humans can even learn to control their brain-waves, using electroencephalogram (EEG) biofeedback.

The nature of biofeedback includes auditory, tactile or visual signals. For example, a tone is commonly used in measuring heart rate and this increases and decreases in pitch as heart rate accelerates and decreases respectively. With training, people can then voluntarily control their heart rate in response to these cues. In the clinical field, the use of electromyography (EMG) feedback measures activity in the skeletal muscles by measuring the electrical discharge in muscle fibres. This is recorded by attaching electrodes to the surface of the skin over the muscles to be monitored. The level of activity reflects the degree of tension or relaxation of the muscles and this can be used to identify muscle problems (e.g. facial spasms or muscle tics) or assess treatment success. Temperature biofeedback can also be used to measure stress (see Chapter 8) since high levels of stress tend to constrict blood vessels and raise skin temperature. Relaxation has the opposite effect, opening blood vessels and lowering skin temperature. This form of feedback has been used to successfully treat migraine headaches and *Reynaud's disease* (a vasoconstrictive disorder resulting in constricted blood flow to the fingers or toes).

EVALUATION OF BIOFEEDBACK

- Biofeedback often requires expensive technology and well-trained personnel. Purchasing decisions often equate these costs with measurable benefits in a cost-efficient NHS.
- In addition, benefits derived from biofeedback must result specifically from the treatment itself in demonstrating effectiveness, and

**65**

not some other component of the treatment. Improvements may occur, for example, through the associated relaxation, suggestion or even a placebo effect (e.g. based on an expectation that the treatment will lead to recovery).

- Biofeedback is a specific intervention that should distinguish benefits from general techniques such as relaxation. If all modes of biofeedback decrease **sympathetic nervous system** arousal, then they are comparable to general relaxation techniques or behaviour therapy in terms of effectiveness.
- Evidence suggests that biofeedback is effective for both pain relief and stress, whether used on its own or in combination with other treatments (Brannon and Feist, 1997)

## 8 Behaviour modification

Behaviour modification works on the basis of operant techniques and aims to shape or change behaviour rather than the feelings associated with it. It is difficult to assess the effectiveness of these techniques in treating pain or stress, due in part to the nature of these conditions. Instead, pain behaviours are identified and appropriately reinforced. Fordyce (1974) observed that responses to pain, and pain behaviours, were frequently reinforced in pain patients. This may arise from attention from practitioners or sympathy from family members for example. Treatment programmes were designed to withhold re-inforcers for less desirable pain behaviours (e.g. moaning, grimacing) and reward desired pain behaviours (e.g. engaging in suitable physical activity). Records of observations and assessment of progress against specific criteria (e.g. range of motion, length of sitting tolerance, etc.) enabled progress to be monitored over time and in response to specific interventions.

### EVALUATION OF BEHAVIOUR MODIFICATION

- Behaviour modification has been demonstrated to be effective in improving mobility in pain patients (Fordyce, 1974), although such studies often involve only single-subject designs which limit generalisation of findings.
- A lack of adequate controls in these studies also makes comparisons with other techniques difficult to achieve. Those studies that

have reviewed effectiveness have shown that the use of behaviour modification results in an increase in the level of the pain patient's activity levels and a decrease in their use of medication (Turner and Chapman, 1982a, b).

### 9 Cognitive-behavioural therapy

Although this technique still uses reinforcement, the emphasis here is on using intrinsic reinforcers (e.g. self-reinforcers) to change cognitions and behaviours. The assumption here is that, by changing a pain patient's perception and thoughts about an event (e.g. their interpretation and meaning of being 'in pain'), then this may also change their emotional and physiological reactions to pain. This therapy is based on Ellis's (1962) research into *rational emotive therapy* (which works on changing or eradicating irrational thoughts) and Bandura's (1977) research into *self-efficacy* (encouraging beliefs about confidence in changing pain thoughts and behaviour). Pain patients are given cognitive strategies to manage their pain more effectively. For example, in *inoculation training*, patients are taught to construct a mental immunity to their pain by thinking differently about the source of their pain experience. These techniques are combined with relaxation and controlled breathing skills. Dolce (1987) showed that self-efficacy in pain patients predicted their treatment success. Patients who failed to show increases in self-efficacy during treatment and who attributed improvements to external factors (e.g. the therapist or the programme) rather than their own skills and abilities were less likely to implement the techniques they had learned for managing their pain problem. They were also at a higher risk of relapse.

#### EVALUATION OF COGNITIVE-BEHAVIOURAL THERAPY

- As with behaviour modification techniques, assessment of the effectiveness of cognitive-behaviour therapy is difficult because of the different samples, techniques, and procedures involved.
- In contrast with behaviour modification techniques, cognitive–behavioural therapy tends to bring less noticeable short-term changes in behaviour, although it appears to be more successful in terms of producing permanent improvements in the alleviation of pain.

- Cognitive-behaviour therapy appears to be even more effective when used in combination with other techniques such as relaxation treatments. These findings depend to some extent on the location and intensity of pain experienced and so generalisations are difficult to make here.

## Multimodal approaches

Multimodal approaches not only combine different treatments but also use different modes of delivery (e.g. visual, auditory, tactile) for the pain patient and therefore have different outcome measures of effectiveness. As stated above, evidence suggests that combining different treatments and approaches to the treatment of pain has yielded promising results. For example, Blanchard *et al.* (1990) used a multimodal approach to compare the effectiveness of the following four treatment groups in treating tension headache: a progressive muscle relaxation group, a group using progressive muscle relaxation combined with cognitive therapy group, a pseudo (false) meditation group and a control group. The first two experimental groups reported significant improvement over the last two control groups on a headache index and significant reduction in use of medication. However, the mechanisms of pain relief involving combined treatments and therapies such as these are still relatively unknown. More research is required to identify which kinds of treatments are most effective for particular types of pain experience.

## Multidisciplinary treatments: the pain clinic

Extending the use of multimodal approaches further in the treatment of pain, pain clinics have recently been set up that adopt a multi-disciplinary approach to the treatment of pain. Pain clinics do not necessarily operate solely in a hospital or clinical setting but in *any* context within which pain is managed and treated. The clinics aim to focus on those factors that cause or exacerbate pain and then set appropriate goals for each patient. Treatment is wide-ranging and may include improving physical and lifestyle functioning (e.g. by improving muscle tone, self-esteem and self-efficacy or reducing boredom, inappropriate pain behaviours and other secondary gains arising out of 'being in pain'). In addition, pain clinics aim to reduce over-reliance on drugs by increasing personal control and self-efficacy in such situations. Finally, pain clinics work with the patient's family to help increase **social support** and promote optimism in the pain patient and reduce boredom, anxiety and sick-role behaviours.

## Summary

We have seen that the measurement of pain is a difficult issue. A range of physiological measures have been developed which appear to measure some aspects of pain, although these may be questioned in terms of their reliability and validity. Behavioural assessment of pain is a complementary measure that focuses on the pain behaviours of the pain patient, and uses behaviourist theory to suggest how pain behaviours may be reinforced in the patient. Self-report measures of pain include rating scales and pain questionnaires. We have also seen how varied the medical and psychological treatments for pain can be, depending on the type of pain experienced and the theoretical position adopted. Most pain conditions are now treated with a combination of medical and psychological approaches, making this distinction now less appropriate. The wider acceptance of the biopsychosocial model of health (outlined in the first chapter), together with the use of multimodal approaches in treating pain and the growth in pain clinics all support this initiative.

## Further reading

Brannon, L. and Feist, J. (1997) *Health Psychology*, Pacific Grove, CA: Brooks Cole. This excellent textbook reviews many of these research areas in more detail and considers a wider range of treatments that are available for understanding and treating pain.

Cave, S. (1999) *Therapeutic Approaches in Psychology*, London: Routledge. This modular series text outlines a range of therapeutic approaches, many of which may be used for understanding and treating pain, including hypnosis and cognitive behaviour therapy.

Skevington, S. M. (1995) *The Psychology of Pain*, Chichester: Wiley. This textbook considers the management and treatment of pain from a very wide perspective, and follows the reader through a developmental process from the initial experience of pain, through the consultation and treatment process, personal coping and the effects of pain on both patients and carers.

# 5

# Doctor–patient communication

◈ The patient–practitioner relationship
◈ Compliance with medical advice
◈ Psychological aspects of hospitalisation
◈ Preparation for surgery
◈ Summary

## The patient–practitioner relationship

The doctor–patient relationship is considered by the World Health Organization (WHO, 1993) as the cornerstone of good medical practice and is a very important area in health psychology for many reasons. First, research suggests that 60–80 per cent of medical diagnoses are made on the basis of information arising from the medical interview alone, as are a similar proportion of treatment decisions (WHO, 1993). Second, research suggests that doctors and patients do not always share the same view of the success (or otherwise!) of the consultation process. Often, doctors are over-optimistic about how well the consultation went and how likely it is the advice offered will be acted upon. Third, the doctor–patient relationship is of critical importance in terms of enhancing compliance to medical requests (helping patients to take the required medication (and/or advice) at the right times, in the right amounts, etc.). Finally, the exchange of information between doctor and patient, including perhaps the breaking of bad news, is of primary concern here. Doctors who may not be well trained in delivering such information may make an already distressed patient worse through a lack of tact and sensitivity in managing the consultation process. Consider the following quotations from a patient and doctor to illustrate these points:

### PATIENTS ON DOCTORS

'He'll say well, we'll talk about it next time. And next time he'll talk fast, he out-talks you – and rushes out of the room and then when he's out of the room you think, well, I was supposed to ask him what he's going to do about my medicine . . . you run in the hall and he has disappeared that fast.' (Tagliacozzo and Mauksh, 1972, cited in E. G. Jaco (ed.), *Patients, Physicians and Illness* (2nd edn, pp. 172–85), New York: Free Press.)

### DOCTORS ON PATIENTS

'What must I tell the patient? How much of what I learned about him should he know? What words shall I use to convey this information? How much of what I propose to tell him will he understand? How will he react? How much of my advice will he take? What degree of pressure am I entitled to apply?' (Royal College of General Practitioners, *The Future General Practitioner*, 1972, p. 17.)

(Both quotes reprinted from OXCEB A level psychology exam Paper 5; 18 June 1996.)

## Research into doctor–patient communication

*The importance of good communication*

Evans *et al.* (1991, cited in WHO, 1993) found that after taking part in a communication skills course, medical students were more proficient at detecting and responding appropriately to patients' verbal *and* non-verbal cues, and were able to elicit more relevant information from patients. Evans *et al.* demonstrated that students who took part in this course were better at making diagnoses because they were able to elicit full, relevant data from patients, even though they took longer to elicit the information than their control group counterparts. Effective diagnosis, therefore, does not depend solely on identifying physical symptoms of illness but depends also on wider psychological and social factors and these may require different treatment plans. Such positive effects of communication skills training for medical students have been found worldwide (Moorhead, 1992, cited in WHO, 1993) although there is evidence that such training is not being given an important place in medical training in British medical schools (Frederikson and Bull, 1992, cited in WHO, 1993).

In contrast to the benefits of effective communication skills training courses, Beckman and Frankel (1984) demonstrated the effects of poor communication in a sample of doctors during seventy-four different office visits by their patients. Remarkably, in only 23 per cent of the cases did the patient have the opportunity to finish his or her explanation of concerns. In 69 per cent of the visits, the physician interrupted, directing the patient toward a particular disorder. Further, doctors were found to interrupt their patients after they had spoken for an average of only 18 seconds! Beckman and Frankel argue that such 'controlling' techniques not only prevent patients from discussing their concerns but may also lead to the loss of important information that would aid diagnosis. In evaluating this study, it could also be argued that, since doctors knew that these consultations were being recorded, this study might actually underestimate the real extent of this problem.

*Doctors' use of jargon and technical language*

Many studies suggest that patients understand relatively few of the complex terms that doctors use. It is estimated that a newly registered GP will probably have acquired more than 13,000 new words or terms that, during patient consultations, may appear baffling to the patient. One example is provided below:

'When my first child was born, the doctor kept coming in every day and asking "have you voided?". So I'd say "No". So in comes the nurse with some paraphernalia that was scary. So I said, "What the devil are you going to do?". And she said, "I'm going to catheterize you, you haven't voided." Well, of course, I knew what catheterization was. I said, "You are going to play hell. I've peed every day since I've been here." [The nurse explained that the doctor had told her the patient hadn't voided.] I said, "Is that what he said?" And she said, "Of course Rusty, didn't you know?" And I said, "Well of course, why didn't he just ask me if I'd peed? I'd have told him."'

(Samora *et al.*, 1961 cited in Taylor, 1995: 348–449)

Taylor (1995) suggests that doctors may use jargon-filled language to stop the patient asking too many questions or to keep the patient from discovering that the doctor is not certain what the patient's problem is. Whatever the reasons, the use of over-complex language can create a barrier to effective doctor–patient communication. WHO (1993) recommended the following in doctor–patient consultations:

- During patient consultations, doctors should monitor the level of jargon they use rather than abandon it. In particular, doctors should monitor how best to explain the diagnosis to patients, giving reasons behind such diagnosis together with suggestions for management of this condition, again accompanied by reasons.
- Doctors should also monitor the use of potentially frightening words like 'cancer' or 'lump' even when used in a negative sense (e.g. 'We can rule out cancer') since this may raise more fears than it allays, especially if this diagnosis had never occurred to the patient.
- Doctors should also monitor the certainty with which they give advice so that their patients are not left misled by spurious (false) certainty or left uneasy by apparent doubt in the doctor's mind. A balance of confidence is required when doctors give advice or make clinical diagnoses.

### Making a diagnosis

Clinical decision-making processes are a specialised form of problem solving that often uses inductive reasoning. This involves collecting evidence and data to develop a hypothesis. The doctor (or other health professional), in making an informed diagnosis, makes use of signs and symptoms provided by the patient. Within this framework, a GP would begin a consultation with a patient without any prior model of that patient's problem. They would then ask the appropriate questions regarding the patient's history and symptoms and then develop a hypothesis about the problem presented. In reality, however, a doctor's clinical decision-making is more similar to the hypothetico-deductive model of decision-making in which a number of specific hypotheses are developed early on in the consultation process and then tested by the doctor's selection of questions (Weinman, 1987).

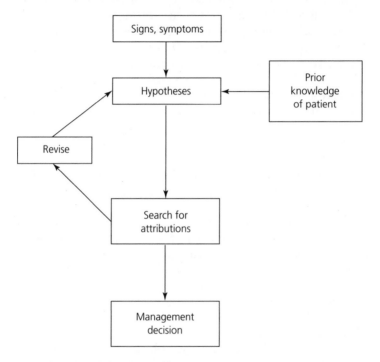

*Figure 5.1* **Clinical decision-making**

*Source:* Originally titled 'Diagnosis as a form of problem-solving'. From *An Outline of Psychology as Applied to Medicine*, (p.186) by J. Weinman 1987. Reprinted by permission of Butterworth Heinemann Publishers, a division of Reed Educational & Professional Publishing Ltd.

The above model of stages in diagnostic problem-solving (Weinman, 1987) involves a series of different stages in which:

• Information is accessed about the patient symptoms (to understand the nature of the problem and form an internal representation of the type of problem presented).

- Hypotheses are developed (about the possible causes, and solutions, of the problem). These hypotheses in turn are influenced by the doctor's approach to health (e.g. the importance they give to the medical model compared with the biopsychosocial model for example). The relative probability of having a certain disease, the seriousness of the disease and how treatable it is are also considered. For example, if a disease is easily treated, and the consequences of not treating it are life-threatening, then it would be a good choice to treat it even if the doctor is not positive about the diagnosis. Finally, the knowledge of the patient is also considered here (e.g. how often they present themselves to the doctor). Doctors are trained to consider the most serious possible diagnoses first. It is often reported that one of a doctor's worst fears is in failing to diagnose a serious condition (e.g. lung cancer rather than a chest cough).
- A search for attributes (which confirms or refutes the original hypothesis). Research suggests that doctors' questioning tends to be biased towards confirming their original hypothesis and that new evidence may even be distorted to support the original hypothesis (Weinman, 1987). Part of this problem is that, like all problem-solvers, clinicians find it difficult to search for negative attributes and instead search for confirmatory evidence (MacWhinney, 1973). For example, an initial hypothesis that a patient has a psychological problem may cause the doctor to focus on the patient's psychological state and ignore the patient's attempts to talk about their physical symptoms.
- Making a management decision (the outcome of the above) results in the doctor's making a decision on the way forward. Weinman (1987) notes that the outcome of a consultation is not an absolute entity but is itself a hypothesis that may be supported or refuted by future events.

### The effects of doctor variability

Doctors may be variable in the above process because they may:

- access different information about a patient's symptoms
- develop different hypotheses about causes and treatments
- access different attributes of the patient's medical condition to confirm or refute hypotheses

- demonstrate different degrees of bias towards seeking to confirm their original diagnosis
- consequently reach different management decisions

All of these factors may play a role in the doctor–patient consultation and indeed the wider doctor–patient relationship. The picture that emerges therefore is that the doctor–patient relationship is very important in terms of helping the decision-making process at each stage and barriers to communication may result in a false diagnosis being made and therefore inappropriate management or treatment regimes may be put in place.

## Compliance with medical advice

Compliance can be defined as 'the extent to which the patient's behaviour (in terms of taking medications, following diets or other lifestyle changes) coincides with medical or health advice' (Haynes *et al.*, 1979). It has become of increasing concern to both health psychologists and medical practitioners as one of the main vehicles to patient recovery and enhancement of positive health. The term 'compliance' has been criticised for carrying an authoritarian ring to it and increasingly in the literature, there is a preferencee for '**adherence**' or even 'therapeutic alliance' to suggest a more co-operative approach on the part of both the patient and the health professional (Pitts and Phillips, 1998). Surprisingly, research evidence suggests that as many as 50 per cent of the patients with chronic illnesses such as diabetes and hypertension (high blood pressure) are not compliant with their medication regimes (Ogden, 1996) and that the level of compliance is not directly related to the seriousness of the disorder. This suggests, therefore, that there may be psychological factors involved in non-compliance with medication.

In addition to these obvious health concerns, there are also financial implications for non-compliance. For example, in 1980, between $396 and $792 million were 'wasted' in the USA because of non-compliance to prescribed drugs (Ogden, 1996). Of course, measuring what is, in essence, the absence of behaviour is particularly problematic and some aspects of non-compliance are more easily measured than others (Pitts and Phillips, 1998).

### *Predicting patient compliance*

Ley (1981, 1989) developed a cognitive hypothesis model of patient compliance which showed that compliance could be predicted by a combination of patient satisfaction with the process of consultation, understanding of the information given and recall of this information, as illustrated in Figure 5.2.

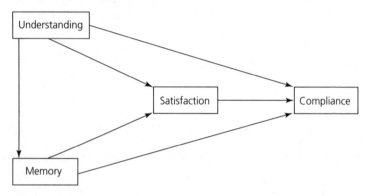

***Figure 5.2*** **Model of patient compliance**

*Source*: Originally titled 'Relationships between understanding, memory satisfaction and compliance'. By P. Ley 'Patients understanding and recall' in D. Pendleton and J. Hasler *Doctor-Patient Communication*, with permission from Academic Press Ltd.

EVALUATION OF LEY'S MODEL OF COMPLIANCE

Brannon and Feist (1997, p. 165) argue that a useful theory or model in health psychology should:

- generate significant research
- organise and explain observations
- help the practitioner predict and change behaviours

Ley's model has satisfied all of the above criteria to some degree, as the following research indicates.

### *Patient satisfaction*

Ley (1988) reviewed 21 studies of hospital patients and found that a total of 28 per cent of general practice patients in the UK were dissatisfied with the treatment they received. Reported dissatisfaction of hospital patients was even higher with 41 per cent dissatisfied with their treatment. Further investigation found that dissatisfaction stemmed from different aspects of the consultation, in particular the affective aspects (e.g. lack of emotional support and understanding), the behavioural aspects (e.g. prescribing, adequate explaining) and competence (e.g. appropriateness of referral, diagnosis) of the health professional. Ley (1989) found that patient satisfaction also included the content of the consultation. In this area, he found that patients were 'information seekers' (i.e. wanted to know as much information as possible about their condition), rather than 'information blunters' (i.e. did not want to know the true seriousness of their condition) even if that meant receiving bad news. These findings have been replicated elsewhere for diagnoses of cancer, where over 85 per cent of patients wanted all information about diagnosis, treatment and prognosis (Kelly and Friesen, 1950; Reynolds *et al.*, 1981). Similarly, in a review of nine studies of terminal illness, 60–98 per cent of patients wanted to know their bad news (Veatch, 1978, cited in Ley, 1982). There is some evidence, however, that a small but significant group do not want to be given the truth for cancer and heart disease (Kubler-Ross, 1969; Hackett and Weisman, 1969). These findings could be due, at least in part, to the attitudes that prevailed during the period in which these studies were conducted. Research suggests that attitudes have changed since the late 1960s and early 1970s towards individuals' wanting to seek more information about their health and illness.

### *Patient understanding*

Compliance is strongly related to patients being able to understand not only the nature of their condition but also the advised treatment regime and the processes involved in such treatment. Boyle (1970) asked patients to define a range of different illnesses using a checklist and found that only 85 per cent could define arthritis correctly, 80 per cent bronchitis, 77 per cent jaundice and only 52 per cent palpitations. Boyle also asked the patients to locate various organs and found that only 49 per cent could correctly locate the liver, 42 per cent the heart and only 20 per cent the stomach! Other research suggests a need to explain the causality and seriousness of illness as well as location of vital organs. Roth (1979) found that, although patients had a good understanding of causality in terms of smoking behaviour and lung cancer, 50 per cent thought that lung cancer caused by smoking had a good prognosis for recovery when in fact this disease is fatal. Roth also found that 30 per cent of patients thought that hypertension could be cured by treatment when it can only be managed (e.g. through lifestyle changes) rather than cured.

### Patient recall

Patients may report good satisfaction with their consultation and good understanding of their condition, but if they cannot remember their advice, then this will affect compliance rates. Bain (1977) tested recall of a sample of patients who attended a GP practice and found that 37 per cent were unable to recall the name of the drug they had been prescribed, 23 per cent could not recall the frequency of the dose and 25 per cent could not recall the duration of treatment. Crichton *et al.* (1978) found that 22 per cent of patients had forgotten their advised treatment regimes after visiting their GPs. Ley (1989) found that the following psychological factors all increase recall of information in compliance:

- lowering of anxiety
- increased medical knowledge
- higher intellectual level
- importance and frequency of statements
- primacy effects (where we remember most the first thing that is said to us)

Contrary to some stereotypes, however, age has no effect on recall success. These findings are also supported by Homedes (1991) who reports that more than 200 variables have been found to affect compliance. He categorises them as:

- characteristics of the patient
- characteristics of the treatment regime
- features of the disease
- the relationship between the health-care provider and the patient
- the clinical setting

Using research summarised above, and your own knowledge of health psychology, suggest ways in which compliance may be improved in a female patient, aged 32 years, with diabetes, who works full-time and has recently completed an A-level in Human Biology through attending evening class at a local college. Consider the importance of oral vs. written information, primacy effects, level of information and stress factors in your recommendation. Try to find research that supports your recommendations.

*Progress exercise*

## Psychological aspects of hospitalisation

Most people living in industrialised societies will be admitted to hospital at least once in their lives and, for a few, hospitalisation may be a regular feature of their lives (Pitts and Phillips, 1998). Hospitalisation brings with it changes in daily routines and a loss of privacy and independence. Taylor (1995) investigated the psychological effects of hospitalisation on patients and found that, from the moment of admission, patients experience anxiety over their illness or disorder, confusion over the prospect of hospitalisation and concern over the role obligations they must leave behind unfulfilled. At the same time, the patient is expected to be helpful, co-operative and 'act out' their dependent role without being too demanding, whilst also being physically confined in the hospital ward! They may show a variety of psychological symptoms whilst in hospital, most notably anxiety and depression. Concern over test results or surgery may produce insomnia (disturbed sleeping patterns), terrifying nightmares and an inability to concentrate.

In addition, communication between patients and staff may further add to anxieties, particularly if information is withheld by staff from the patient because of possible fear of misinterpretation or further anxiety. Such disorientation and lack of communication may result in the patient's adopting the *hospital patient role* which is the result of this socialisation process (Taylor, 1995). Their major task is to please the doctor and nursing staff by behaving appropriately, following instructions and co-operating fully with hospital expectations and norms. Staff reinforce this 'good patient' role and the passive, undemanding and co-operative behaviours that go with it. In contrast, 'bad patients' may frequently ask questions, complain or query their treatment. Reactions to such patients may depend on the severity of their illness. Whilst the seriously ill are often forgiven their complaints, patients who complain and are not seriously ill arouse considerable irritation in staff (Leiderman and Grisso, 1985).

A number of researchers have argued that being a 'good patient' may not always be the most effective path for recovery since they do not take an active role in their own care and may fail to report new or changing patterns of symptoms (Pitts and Phillips, 1998). Such passivity may develop into feelings of **learned helplessness**, where patients learn that they cannot change the situation they are in (Seligman, 1975).

Finally, reactions to hospitalisation may not be helped by the 'dependent language culture' that exists between patients and their carers. Language style may be well meant but received in a nursery school context. Patients are invited to 'pop' in and out of bed, 'slip off their clothes' and 'be a good chap'. Language use is never neutral and, in this context, may be viewed by both patient and practitioner as maintaining or even enhancing the differences in roles. Clearly psychology has a significant role to play in highlighting these interpersonal and communicative issues and suggesting ways in which reassurance can be expressed or requested in a mutually respectful manner.

## Preparation for surgery

If hospitalisation brings with it all of the above attendant problems, then preparation for surgery and other stressful medical procedures includes all of these and many more issues to consider. The amount and kind of preparation offered and given has varied a great deal depending on the nature of hospital setting, type of surgery and patient characteristics. Surgery involves a combination of experience of anaesthetic, anticipation of pain and incision using needles or knives. Each of these events is stressful by itself but, used in combination, may be particularly difficult to anticipate and cope with (Pitts and Phillips, 1998).

Preparation for surgery has made use of a variety of clinical ratings (e.g. ratings of anxiety), physical indices (e.g. blood pressure) and pre-operative medication (e.g. analgesics which reduce pain). Of central importance to all of these measures is the presentation of information to the patient and this may be of two main types:

- Procedural information: the patient is informed about the procedures to be undertaken, including the time of day and length of operation.
- Sensory information: the patient is informed of the likely sensations they can expect to experience, such as the nature and duration of pain.

In addition, the patient is given instructions on behaviours that will promote effective recovery (e.g. bed-rest, light exercise, etc.) and possible behaviours to avoid (e.g. scratching, smoking, etc.). This of course will vary with the type and nature of surgery.

Research suggests that awareness of individual differences (e.g. personality differences) in preparing for surgery may be useful (Pitts and Phillips, 1998). Knowledge of patient characteristics may help health professionals to target an appropriate amount of information at the right level for patients in order to reduce their anxiety and promote understanding. Similarly, patients differ in terms of their preferred coping style (cognitive and behavioural efforts to manage a stressful event) in response to the prospect of surgery. Some patients may be 'information seekers' and demand information about all aspects of their surgery, whilst others may be 'information blunters' and prefer not to be informed about their surgery. Recent evidence suggests a shift towards the former category of patients.

The benefits of effective preparation for surgery are both physiological and psychological. Physiological benefits include a reduction in stress which in turn decreases sympathetic nervous system arousal and related improvements in **immune system** function. Psychological benefits include a reduction in anxiety and depression and an increased level of personal control. All of these benefits in turn promote effective recovery.

---

Imagine that you are to be admitted to hospital tomorrow to undergo minor surgery. It is likely that you will be in hospital for one week. List all of your major concerns that you might have relating to (a) the social, psychological and environmental factors that may cause you anxiety whilst in hospital and (b) your concerns about the surgery itself. How might psychologists help to make this experience less stressful?

Review exercise

## Summary

We have seen the importance of effective communication in the patient–practitioner relationship and the role that health psychology may play in this area. Patient satisfaction and compliance are determined by many factors, some of them psychological in nature. Hospitalisation and surgery are sources of stress for most people. Psychology can play a key role here in terms of helping to recognise signs of distress and anxiety in patients. Invasive medical procedures need careful preparation to reduce anxiety and depression and help promote recovery. Interventions may include the use of clinical ratings, physical indices and pre-operative medication.

The provision of information to the patient is central to this process. The nature and extent of information giving should be carefully considered and tailored to meet the needs and demands of the patient. Above all, this chapter shows that patients are uniquely human and have to be treated with sensitivity, respect and understanding if treatment is to be effective and recovery is to be promoted. A focus of medical practitioners on physical or medical factors alone is not sufficient for effective patient care and the 'best doctors' or 'best nurses' are considered as those who have these valuable psychological skills of communication, caring and knowledge.

## Further reading

Ogden, J. (1996) *Health Psychology: A Textbook*, Buckingham: Open University Press. This text provides a thorough review of doctor–patient communication and the role of health professionals' health beliefs.

Pitts, M. and Phillips, K. (eds) (1998) 2nd edn. *Health Psychology: An Introduction*, London: Routledge. This text provides two excellent chapters on the medical consultation itself together with the experience of treatment, both of which contain a wide range of contemporary research in this area.

Taylor, S. E. (1995) *Health Psychology*, New York: McGraw-Hill. This comprehensive text on health psychology contains two very readable chapters on the use of health services and patient–practitioner interaction which, taken together, provide extensive reading on doctor–patient communication, hospitalisation and preparation for stressful medical procedures.

# 6

# Psychological factors in illness

## The mind–body issue in health

In the first chapter, we considered the nature and assumptions of the medical model and the biopsychosocial model applied to health. Essentially, we saw that the medical model focused on physical causes for health problems (e.g. germs, genes and chemicals) and advocated physical treatments as a result (e.g. drugs). The mind here is considered in physical terms (i.e. as the brain) and thus treating the brain is no different from treating the mind. The biopsychosocial model of health fills a gap in this process by showing how biological, psychological and social factors all interact in health. Whether this involves the issue of mind here remains a controversial issue. At the very least, this model allows for the possibility that non-physical factors influence our health. This issue remains one of the great challenges in health psychology.

In contemporary health psychology, hundreds of studies have suggested that 'mind over matter' can improve our health, help us to lose weight and even 'cure' cancer. The exact mechanisms involved here, however, remain elusive. The concept of 'mind' by definition lacks observability and testability and this has led some behaviourists to reject its existence. Alternatively, many health psychologists suggest that we ignore the power of our mind at our peril. The reported dramatic effects of mental imagery, relaxation training and non-Western healing techniques have suggested that there is more to health than meets the eye, literally! All we need to do is to discover the underlying processes, harness the energy and direct it to improving our health.

## The role of psychological factors in chronic health problems

As discussed in Chapter 2, chronic health problems are typically diseases that cannot be cured, but rather must be managed by the patient and health practitioner together. Examples of chronic health problems include heart disease, cancer, diabetes and arthritis. All of these conditions have psychological factors that are involved in their initial onset, management and treatment. In fact, one could argue that, because these 'modern diseases of living' are multi-factorial in nature (i.e. many factors are involved, including lifestyle), psychology has as significant a role to play in their prevention, management and treatment as medicine itself. This chapter will now focus on the contribution that psychology can make in three important areas of chronic illness and high mortality: HIV/AIDS, cancer and **coronary heart disease (CHD)**.

### Chronic ill-health problems

#### *Acquired immune deficiency syndrome (AIDS)*

The first case of **acquired immune deficiency syndrome (AIDS)** was diagnosed in the USA in 1981 (although it now appears that there may have been isolated cases of AIDS before that date). It was regarded at that time as a disease that was specific to homosexuality and was known as GRIDS (gay-related immune deficiency syndrome). As a result of this false belief, a number of theories were developed to try to explain the occurrence of this new illness among homosexuals.

For example, some theories suggested that AIDS was a response to the overuse of recreational drugs (e.g. 'poppers') or to over-exposure to semen, and they focused on the perceived lifestyles of the homosexual population. In 1982, one year later, AIDS also occurred in haemophiliacs. This forced a shift in focus of then current theories away from lifestyles and towards considering AIDS as a virus. Haemophiliacs could contract such a virus through their use of Factor VIII, a donated blood-clotting agent. In 1984, the human immunodeficiency virus type 1 (HIV 1) was identified, and in 1985 HIV 2 was identified in Africa. The virus appears to be transmitted exclusively by the exchange of cell-containing bodily fluids, especially semen and blood.

The relationship between HIV and AIDS is complex. Transmission routes from HIV to AIDS are still under investigation. We now know that the viral agent involved in AIDS is a retrovirus (a virus containing ribonucleic acid (RNA) that can convert its genetic material into the deoxyribonucleic acid (DNA) of its host's cells, causing cancer or impaired immune system function). This retrovirus is known as the 'human immunodeficiency virus' (HIV) and specifically attacks the helper T-cells and the macrophages in the immune system. The period between contracting the virus and developing the symptoms of AIDS is highly variable, with some individuals developing the symptoms quite quickly and others remaining free of symptoms for up to 8 or 9 years or more. An individual may therefore test HIV seropositive (+) but be free of a diagnosis of AIDS for many years, although they can still pass the virus on to others as above. Some individuals may contract the HIV virus without going on to develop 'full-blown' AIDS.

### *The role of psychology in the study of HIV and AIDS*

HIV is transmitted mostly because of people's behaviour (e.g. sexual intercourse, sharing needles with infected users) and therefore psychology has a key role to play in predicting 'at-risk' individuals (or groups), explaining risk-taking behaviours and managing interventions in this area. In particular, health psychologists believe that an understanding of attitudes and beliefs in this area is influential in changing behaviour. It is acknowledged, however, that attitudes alone may not be a good predictor of behaviour. Wider factors must also be considered in the study of HIV and AIDS, and these include related

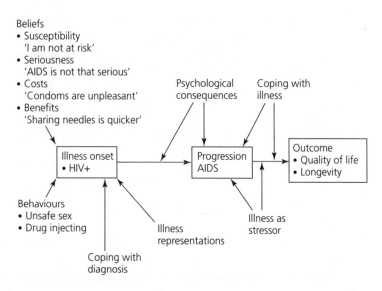

*Figure 6.1* **The role of psychology in HIV and AIDS**

*Source*: Originally titled 'The potential role of Psychology in HIV'. J. Ogden (1996, p. 260) with permission from Open University Press.

issues of susceptibility, progression from HIV to AIDS and longevity. These are summarised in a model proposed by Ogden (1996) showing the potential role of psychology in HIV and AIDS (see Figure 6.1).

This model suggests that different psychological factors may influence different stages in the development of the disease and these are summarised below.

### SUSCEPTIBILITY

Not everyone exposed to the HIV virus becomes HIV-positive. Psychological factors may influence an individual's susceptibility to become HIV positive. For example, some people are physically more susceptible than others, perhaps due to stress etc., and some people deny the risk and therefore fail to take adequate precautions, which increases their risk. Research into attitudes mentioned above suggests that there are not only individual differences in attitudes towards HIV and AIDS (for example, within a group of injecting drug users) but also changes in attitudes across time. Indeed, studies in the UK of the relationship between perception of risk and knowledge of HIV and AIDS suggest that, although knowledge about the transmission of HIV was high, many college students reported being relatively invulnerable to AIDS (Abrams *et al.*, 1990). Beliefs about 'denial of risk' range from the symptoms not being evident, their partners not being promiscuous and even their partners coming from geographical areas that were not considered to be of high risk. This supports Weinstein's (1984) research in health psychology, which showed that many 'risk-taking' individuals are 'unrealistic optimists' (have a strong belief that it will not happen to them). This may be based on a lack of personal experience with the problem or a belief that the problem is preventable by their own action. Individuals may also believe that the problem will not appear in the future because it has not appeared so far or believe that the problem is infrequent. All of these factors may apply to HIV and AIDS. Health educational campaigns have therefore attempted to change attitudes and behaviour by encouraging the practice of safe sex (e.g. through condom use) although it is now acknowledged that promoting safer sex is more complicated than simply increasing knowledge and providing services.

## PROGRESSION

The time in progression from HIV to AIDS is variable. Psychological factors may play a role in promoting the replication of the HIV virus. For example, it is suggested that injecting drugs further stimulates the immune system and that replication of the virus may be influenced by further exposure to the HIV virus. In addition, contact with drugs that may have an immunosuppressive effect (i.e. reduce effectiveness of the immune system further), or other viruses such as herpes complex, may also promote replication of the virus. Sodroski *et al.* (1984) suggested that stress or distress may also promote replication of the virus, causing quicker progression from HIV to AIDS. Psychology has a clear role to play here in terms of limiting progression of the disease, for example through discouraging social homophobia (therefore reducing distress in homosexuals) or discouraging drug misuse and further risky behaviours for those who have already contracted HIV.

## LONGEVITY

Not everyone with HIV dies from AIDS. Psychological factors and interventions may promote longevity through encouraging positive beliefs and promoting healthy behaviours. Research suggests that such factors may influence the state of **immunosuppression** of the individual, although the exact mechanisms through which this operates are not clear. For example, Solomon *et al.* (1987 cited in Ogden, 1996) followed up twenty-one AIDS patients and found that their survival could be predicted by:

- their general health status at baseline (the time they contracted the disease);
- their health behaviours;
- level of **hardiness** (Kobasa *et al.*, 1982) (a coping style based on having high levels of personal *control*); *commitment* (e.g. finding meaning in their work, values and personal relationships) and *challenge* (seeing potentially stressful events as a challenge);
- the level of social support (e.g. psychological support from friends, relatives, etc.);
- Type C behaviour (self-sacrificing, self-blaming, not emotionally expressive);
- coping strategies (e.g. emotion-focused and problem-focused strategies).

A follow-up study by Solomon and Temoshok (1987 cited in Ogden, 1996) suggested that Type C behaviour was not related to longevity although expression of anger and hostility did contribute to a positive outcome. Both of these studies, however, although prospective in nature, involved only small sample sizes. This restricts the extent to which these findings can be generalised to similar populations.

### *Interim summary*

The study of HIV and AIDS illustrates the role and value of psychology at different stages of an illness. Psychological factors are important not only in terms of understanding attitudes and beliefs about HIV and AIDS but also in influencing 'at-risk' behaviours, an individual's susceptibility to contracting the virus, the speed of replication of the virus once contracted and even an individual's subsequent longevity.

### Coronary heart disease (CHD)

'Coronary heart disease' is a general term that refers to illnesses caused by **atherosclerosis** (narrowing of the coronary arteries which are the vessels that supply the heart with blood). When these vessels become constricted or blocked, the flow of oxygen and nourishment to the heart becomes partially or completely obstructed. Temporary shortages of oxygen and nourishment frequently cause pain. This is called 'angina pectoris' and this pain radiates across the chest and arm. When severe shortages of oxygen and nourishment occur, this may result in a **myocardial infarction** or heart attack.

Research suggests that many factors may contribute towards heart disease (Ogden, 1996). It is particularly common among males and the elderly (responsible for 33 per cent of deaths in men under 65 years of age and 28 per cent of all deaths). It also has a family component, being more common among the offspring of individuals who have had heart disease. Known risk factors include high blood pressure, diabetes, cigarette smoking, obesity, high serum cholesterol level and low levels of physical activity.

### The role of psychology in CHD

Some of the above factors are more easily modified than others and psychological factors may play a key role in this process. This may include predicting and changing behavioural risk factors or the rehabilitation of sufferers, for example (Ogden, 1996).

#### PREDICTING AND CHANGING BEHAVIOURAL RISK FACTORS

This may include helping individuals to stop smoking. Ogden (1996) reports that smoking 20 cigarettes per day increases the risk of CHD in middle age three-fold and stopping smoking can reduce the risk of a second heart attack by 50 per cent. In addition, dietary changes that reduce intake of saturated fat and increase dietary fibre are also known to help protect against heart disease. High blood pressure, a risk factor for CHD, may be influenced by genetic factors, obesity,

**91**

excess alcohol intake and excess salt consumption. Similarly, high levels of stress with low social support and low perceived control are also implicated in heart disease (Karasek and Theorell, 1990). Finally, Friedman and Rosenman's (1959) classic study into personality and heart disease initially suggested that a person with a Type A behaviour pattern (characterised by excessive competitiveness, time urgency and hostility) was more at risk of CHD than a Type B behaviour profile (relaxed, quieter, no time urgency). Subsequent research which sought to test this link between personality and heart disease, however, has either failed to replicate these findings or resulted in the need to consider other variables that might *mediate* this relationship (e.g. age and job-type may moderate these effects). The relationship here is more complex than at first proposed.

Psychology has also made a significant contribution here in terms of encouraging CHD sufferers to modify their risk factors against a recurrent heart attack by changing the above risk factors of exercise, Type A behaviour, smoking and diet. Contrary to some beliefs, experiencing and surviving a heart attack does not necessarily increase the risk of a recurrent attack (reinfarction). Indeed, Friedman *et al.* (1986) in a five-year longitudinal study involving 1,000 participants who had all suffered a heart attack, showed how a Type A behaviour modification programme reduced the risk of a recurrent heart attack in comparison to a control group. The programme focused on discussing the participant's beliefs and the values of Type A behaviours, reducing work demands, practising relaxation techniques and changing the participant's cognitive framework. This study showed not only that could Type A behaviour be modified but also that, when it is modified, it could serve as a protective function against recurrent heart attacks (reinfarction).

## Terminal illness

### Cancer

Cancer is defined as any malignant tumour and arises from the abnormal and uncontrolled division of cells that invade and destroy

Using the above research findings, design a brief treatment regime for Steve, a single 38-year-old business executive, who has recently suffered a myocardial infarction (heart attack). He is 5 feet 6 inches (1.68 m) tall, weighs 13 stone (82.5 kgs), smokes ten cigarettes a day, and is convinced that working 60 hours per week is the only way to achieve happiness, wealth and prosperity!

the surrounding tissues. There are two types of tumours: *benign* tumours, which do not spread throughout the body, and *malignant* tumours, which show metastasis (the process of cells breaking off from the tumour and moving elsewhere). There are three types of cancer cells: *carcinomas*, which constitute 90 per cent of all cancer cells that originate in tissue cells; *sarcomas*, which originate in connective tissue; and *leukaemias*, which originate in the blood.

### Prevalence of cancer

In 1991, it was reported that there were 6 million new cases of cancer in the world every year, and that one-tenth of all deaths in the world are caused by cancer (Ogden, 1996). In the UK, cancers are the joint leading cause of death with coronary heart disease and together these chronic diseases account for approximately half of all deaths. Within this data, there appear to be gender differences in cancer mortality: women are more susceptible to breast cancer (20 per cent mortality rate), whilst men are more susceptible to lung cancer (36 per cent mortality rate). While the overall incidence of cancer deaths does not appear to be rising, the incidence of lung cancer in women has risen steadily over the last few years, due in part to comparatively larger decreases in smoking among men.

### The role of psychology in cancer

Although the palliative influence (i.e. as a temporary relief rather than a cure) of psychology on cancer was first suggested by Galen in AD 200–300, it was not until recently that this relationship has been studied systematically. Eighty-five per cent of cancers are thought to be potentially avoidable and the discipline of psychology therefore has an exciting contribution to make at all stages of the illness. Indeed, psychology can help mitigate against developing cancer in the first place. Cancer cells are present in most people although not everybody gets cancer. This suggests that there are individual differences in susceptibility to developing cancer. Lifestyle and other factors may trigger the onset of cancer. For example, evidence suggests a strong link between smoking and lung cancer although not every heavy smoker develops lung cancer. The relationship that emerges here is one of probabilities rather than a simple cause-and-effect relationship.

In addition to the above, all those who have cancer do not show progression towards death at the same rate. Consistent with our discussion of HIV and AIDS above, psychology may play an important role in limiting the progression of cancer. Similarly, not all cancer sufferers die of cancer. Psychology may even be involved in promoting longevity following cancer. These factors are summarised in a model proposed by Ogden (1996) showing the potential role of psychology in cancer (see Figure 6.2).

This model suggests that different psychological factors may influence different stages in the development of the disease. These are summarised below.

### INITIATION AND PROMOTION OF CANCER

Behaviour may influence the initiation and promotion of cancer. For example, Smith and Jacobson (1989) reported that 30 per cent of all cancers are related to tobacco use, 35 per cent to diet, 7 per cent to reproductive and sexual behaviour and 3 per cent to alcohol. Stress (see Chapter 8) may also play a role in both the initiation and promotion of cancer, although this has so far only been demonstrated in animal experiments using cancer-prone mice, for example. Studies of stressful life events involving humans have revealed only correlational data, although reliable patterns were found between families who had a cancer victim and stressful life-events including divorce, moving house and deterioration of health (Jacobs and Charles, 1980). Other psychological factors that may be implicated in cancer include the level of perceived control over stressors, coping styles, chronic mild stress (not clinical depression), a Type C personality (see above)

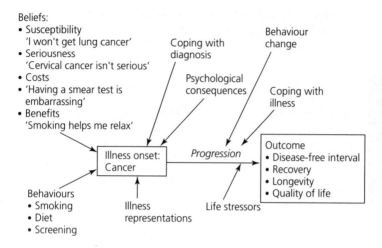

**Figure 6.2** The role of psychology in cancer

*Source*: Originally titled 'The potential role of psychology in cancer'. J. Ogden (1996, p. 268) with permission from Open University Press.

and a low hardiness profile. Of most significant importance here, research by Shaffer *et al*. (1987) showed that medical students who had a Type C personality were over a 30-year period sixteen times more likely to develop cancer than those who did not.

PSYCHOLOGICAL RESPONSES TO CANCER

Emotional responses to cancer include severe depression, grief, lack of control, personality change, anger and anxiety, and this can occur in up to 20 per cent of cancer patients. It is interesting to note here that, at least with operable breast cancer, the emotional state of the sufferers appears to be unrelated to the type of surgery they have. More obvious predictors of emotional responses to cancer include previous psychiatric history, lack of social support, age and lack of an intimate relationship. With advanced cancer, the patient's psychological health was closely related to their physical health (Pinder *et al*., 1993). In addition to emotional responses to cancer, cognitive responses suggest that having a 'fighting spirit' is negatively correlated to anxiety and depression (i.e. a strong 'fighting spirit' wards off anxiety and depression). Again, the reason why this occurs is not known although the biopsychosocial model of health discussed earlier may suggest some answers here.

Progress exercise

How might the biopsychosocial model of health contribute to the management and treatment of cancer? In what ways could the 'fighting spirit' outlined above feature in such a model? How might your views here be tested?

## PSYCHOLOGICAL STRATEGIES FOR COPING

Conversely, beliefs about 'fatalism' (my cancer is inevitable), '**helplessness**' (there's nothing I can do about having cancer) and 'anxious preoccupation' (e.g. intrusive thoughts about the cancer) are all related to lowered mood. Taylor's (1983) study of how women with breast cancer coped with their situation showed three effective strategies. First, they engaged in a search for meaning of how they came to develop cancer (ranging from hereditary factors to stress). Second, they developed a sense of mastery over their illness by believing that they could control it (and any relapses). Finally, they began a process of self-enhancement in which they used social comparison with significant others in their lives to analyse their own condition. They showed 'downward social comparison' by comparing themselves with people who were worse off than they were, thus enhancing self-esteem and improving their own beliefs about their situation. Taylor's 'theory of cognitive adaptation' thus involves a combination of meaning, mastery and self-enhancement in producing effective coping strategies for illness.

## DEALING WITH SYMPTOMS OF CANCER

Psychology has also contributed to the alleviation of symptoms of cancer and in promoting quality of life. Cancer sufferers may experience a range of symptoms, including very distressing pain (affecting about two-thirds of all cancer patients), breathing difficulties, vomiting, sleeplessness, loss of bowel and bladder control, loss of appetite and mental confusion. The following psychosocial interventions have been used to help relieve some of these symptoms:

- pain management (e.g. the use of biofeedback and hypnosis)
- social support interventions (e.g. support groups that emphasise control and meaningful activities)
- treatment of nausea and vomiting (e.g. the use of relaxation and guided imagery – see Chapter 4)
- body-image counselling (building on quality-of-life issues and grief counselling at losing various parts of their body)
- cognitive adaptation strategies (using psychological strategies aimed at improving self-worth)
- holistic treatment (Simonton and Simonton (1975) used relaxation, mental imagery and exercise programmes in the treatment of cancer, focusing on treating the whole person, not just the diseased part of the body).

### LONGEVITY AND PROMOTING A DISEASE-FREE INTERVAL

Although there is no direct relationship between psychological factors and longevity, there appear to be trends from a variety of research that indicate the importance of psychology in this area. First, research by Greer *et al.* (1979) using breast cancer patients found that women who reported a 'fighting spirit' or a 'denial' towards their cancer had a significantly longer disease-free period than the 'helpless' group (who reported that they believed nothing could be done about their illness). These differences persisted over fifteen years, suggesting robust psychological factors here, although the exact nature of this process remains speculative. Indeed, the 'deniers' may have been using different (although equally effective) coping strategies from the 'fighting spirit' group. In addition, important physiological prognostic measures (e.g. **lymph node** involvement in the **lymphatic system**) were not controlled for in this study and this may have affected the results. Further, a case control (**cross-sectional study**) comparing 50 women who had developed their first occurrence of breast cancer with a matched group of another 50 women in remission found that life events rated as severe were also related to the first occurrence of breast cancer. Such case control studies, however, do not allow us to make cause-and-effect statements here, although these findings remain of interest to health psychologists.

Finally, personality factors and coping style have also been related to longevity. Individuals with a Type C ('cancer-prone') conflict-avoiding/emotional-suppression personality type received cognitive-behavioural therapy focused on dealing with stress. This group had lower mortality rates compared with a matched group of controls who did not receive therapy (Eysenck and Grossarth-Maticek, 1991 cited in Ogden, 1996), suggesting that psychological interventions may improve longevity.

## Adjustment to illness

Patients adjust to their illness in different ways. Adjustment is a process that involves a period of time in which patients come to terms with their illness, for example by constructing a personal meaning for their illness and understanding the nature of their illness (causes, consequences and implications). In addition, individuals learn to select appropriate coping mechanisms to help deal effectively with their illness. Within these issues, it is useful to consider that illness does not occur within a social vacuum but rather is a dynamic and interactive process, often affecting family members in different ways for example. Studies of social support (information conveyed from others that one is loved, cared for, valued and esteemed as an integral part of a network) suggest that this may buffer the effects of stress and lead to more effective coping responses following illness (Taylor, 1995). The evidence as to whether social support may reduce the likelihood of serious illness remains equivocal here and some studies even suggest that the provision of social support by spouses in cases of serious illness produces real distress for the carers (Thompson and Pitts, 1992). What emerges here is the notion that chronic illness involves a shared process of adjustment.

The ways in which individuals adjust and adapt to their illness may in itself bring additional problems, challenges and self-insight. In addition, circumstances that result in the loss or immobility of a limb for example (Chapter 4) may also bring profound psychological problems that affect one's **self-image**, identity and confidence. This may be further exacerbated in social situations when patients who are disfigured in some way report initial feelings of being stigmatised and this may be inadvertently amplified by the reactions of others. Other problems of adjustment and adaptation apply to health conditions that may not be visible but are equally demanding in different ways.

Long-term chronic illnesses such as AIDS, cancer and heart disease often bring about a crisis in people's lives, changing the way patients see themselves, resulting in family hardship and disrupted family dynamics. Chronically ill people have physiological, psychological, social and emotional needs that are different from those of healthy people (rather than deficient). Finding ways to satisfy these needs is part of the coping process. Social and emotional needs may be neglected whilst health practitioners attend to the patient's physical needs and this has led to the development of multidisciplinary care teams that recognise the complex nature of care. Consistent with the models discussed earlier, interventions that consider both psychological and social treatments, rather than simply physical treatments, remain the most valuable option, in terms of both patient recovery and satisfaction.

## Summary

We have seen here that psychological factors play a crucial role in the initiation, progression and treatment of many chronic illnesses and diseases. These modern-day 'diseases of living' have behavioural components which, once identified, can be used to either prevent initial onset of the illness or help manage its successful treatment. Most importantly, the biopsychosocial model has shown us that individuals are not simply machines with physical parts that 'go wrong'. Rather, individuals have psychological and spiritual dimensions that impact on their health states and all of this takes place within a social context. A complete understanding of health psychology cannot afford to ignore these issues and real understanding begins to emerge when we consider how these factors interact with one another.

## Further reading

Ogden, J. (1996) *Health Psychology: A Textbook*, Buckingham: Open University Press. Thorough coverage of the contribution of health psychology to treating chronic illnesses and diseases.

Taylor, S. E. (1995) *Health Psychology*, New York: McGraw-Hill. This text contains four chapters on the management of chronic and terminal illness and presents comprehensive research evidence in this area.

# 7

# Lifestyles and health

◪ Aspects of lifestyle
◈ Exercise and nutrition
◈ Obesity and eating disorders
◣ Summary

## Aspects of lifestyle

In the first chapter, we saw how an understanding of health and health psychology is incomplete when the focus is merely on the absence of disease and illness. Instead, contemporary health psychology emphasises the benefits of positive health states and the related area of health promotion (e.g. Ewles and Simnett, 1995). Within this context, the study of an individual's lifestyle is central to our understanding of health. Lifestyle factors such as taking regular exercise and adopting a healthy diet have become of paramount importance. Within a single generation, there have been dramatic changes in our dietary knowledge and habits. For example, in this country, saturated fatty acids, full-fat milk and red meat are being replaced with low saturated fats, semi-skimmed milk and white meat. In addition, we are being encouraged to reduce our intake of agents that may be harmful to our health (e.g. smoking and alcohol). All of these measures are considered to contribute to a 'healthier' lifestyle.

It is estimated that about 50 per cent of premature deaths in Western countries can be attributed to lifestyle (Hamburg *et al.*, 1982). Smokers, on average, reduce their life expectancy by five years and individuals who lead a sedentary (i.e. non-active) lifestyle by two to three years (Bennett and Murphy, 1997). The question then arises, what is meant exactly by a healthier lifestyle? The answer to this question lies in part with to whom this question is asked. A nutritionist would argue that such measures are designed to enrich our bodies with essential nutrients extracted from foods (carbohydrates, fats, proteins, minerals and vitamins), and maintain optimum calorific intake (i.e. of energy value of foods) necessary for optimal functioning. This would include providing a source of energy, material for growth or substances that regulate growth or energy production. A sports psychologist on the other hand might emphasise the importance of regular and appropriate exercise to maintain physical fitness, ensure muscle strength and endurance, increase flexibility in joints and build aerobic (cardio-respiratory) fitness. Either way, we are considering lifestyles here rather than specific health behaviours (e.g. visiting your GP). With lifestyles, we are considering a whole pattern of behaviours that may be tied into the type of job that an individual has, the culture and sub-culture they feel part of, and the people they live with (Banyard, 1996).

Changing trends and fashions in health may be influenced by wider cultural and sub-cultural factors. For example, the family continues to be one of the main sources of information for our food and diet. Commercial influences of television advertisements on children's food preferences are also known to influence lifestyles, even though a healthy diet may sometimes be under-represented on television (Wadden and Brownell, 1984 cited in Banyard, 1996).

### Research into lifestyles

In a famous epidemiological study, Belloc and Breslow (1972) asked a representative sample of 6,928 residents of Almeda County, California whether they engaged in the following seven health practices:

1  Sleeping seven to eight hours daily
2  Eating breakfast almost every day

3  Never or rarely eating between meals
4  Currently being at or near prescribed height-adjusted weight
5  Never smoking cigarettes
6  Moderate or no use of alcohol
7  Regular physical activity

It was immediately found that good health practices were associated with positive health status (i.e. those residents who followed all of the good practices were in better health than those who failed to do so) and this association was independent of age, sex and economic status (Belloc and Breslow, 1972). Further, follow-up studies after five and a half years and nine and a half years showed that good health practices were associated with longevity (longer life expectancy).

Indeed, men who followed all seven of these health practices had a mortality rate that was only 28 per cent of that for men who followed three or less of these practices. For women, the difference was still there but smaller: mortality rates for those who followed all seven practices was only 43 per cent of that for women who followed three or less practices. This study suggests that a person's health lifestyle can affect how long they live. It is important to note here, however, that it is unlikely that the healthiest of lifestyles will result in our living to be 140 years old because there are natural limits on our life expectancy (Fries *et al.*, 1989). The point here is that healthy lifestyles help people stay fit longer and lead an active life into old age with less likelihood of pain, infirmity or chronic disease.

## Exercise and nutrition

### *Physical exercise*

Although about 70 per cent of all adults in the USA currently engage in some form of leisure-time physical activity (Siegel *et al.*, 1995), most of them do not exercise in a way that enhances their physical health. Exercise in its broadest sense can include hundreds of different types of activities. In physiological terms, however, Brannon and Feist (1997) describe only five different types of exercise, each with different goals, activities and advocates.

## ISOMETRIC EXERCISE

Although the body does not move in isometric exercise, muscles push hard (contract) against each other or against an immovable object and thus gain strength. Because joints do not move, it may not be apparent that exercise is taking place. This exercise technique has been shown to strengthen muscle groups although is not effective for overall conditioning.

## ISOTONIC EXERCISE

This exercise requires both the contraction of muscles and the movement of joints (e.g. weight-lifting). Both muscle strength and endurance may be improved if the programme is sufficiently long-lasting and strenuous. Body-building techniques are based on isotonic exercises, although they tend to emphasise 'improvements' in body appearance rather than improving fitness and health.

## ISOKINETIC EXERCISE

This exercise requires exertion for lifting and additional effort to return to the starting position. This type of exercise requires special-ised equipment, so that it adjusts the amount of resistance according to the amount of force that is applied. Research suggests that this method is more effective than both isometric exercise and isotonic exercise in promoting muscle strength and muscle endurance (Pipes and Wilmore, 1975).

## ANAEROBIC EXERCISE

This exercise involves short, intensive bursts of energy without an increased amount of oxygen (e.g. short-distance running, and soft-ball). Research suggests that such exercises improve speed and endurance, although they do not increase the fitness of the coronary and respiratory systems. Indeed, these exercises may be dangerous for people with coronary heart disease.

## AEROBIC EXERCISE

This refers to any type of exercise that requires dramatically increased oxygen consumption over an extended period of time. An obvious example here is jogging, although many other physical activities can be performed aerobically (e.g. walking, cross-country skiing, dancing, rope skipping, swimming and cycling). Intensity and duration of exercise is very important here in order to promote fitness and prevent harm or damage. Exercise must be of a sufficient intensity to increase the heart rate into a certain range (computed from a formula based on age and the maximum possible heart rate). The heart rate should stay at this elevated level for at least 12 minutes, and preferably 15–30 minutes for the aerobic benefits to work. This type of programme requires elevated oxygen use and provides a workout for both the respiratory system (which provides the necessary oxygen) and the coronary system (which pumps the blood). Since coronary abnormalities may exist without any apparent symptoms, it is always advised to have a medical examination before starting a programme of aerobic exercise. In addition, the use of an **electrocardiogram (ECG)** can detect abnormal cardiac activity during exercise (e.g. irregular heartbeat or insufficient blood supply).

### *Physical benefits of exercise*

There are many benefits from taking part in exercise. It seems intuitively correct that exercise helps us to get or stay physically fit although the relationship between exercise and fitness is quite complex and depends on the duration and intensity of exercise and on the definition of fitness. Overall fitness includes measures of muscle strength, muscle endurance, flexibility and cardiorespiratory (aerobic) fitness. Each of the five types of exercise described above contributes to these different types of fitness although no one type of exercise fulfils all of these requirements. In addition to this, Kuntzleman (1978) makes a distinction between *organic fitness* (our capacity for action and movement determined by inherent factors such as genes, age and health status) and *dynamic fitness*, which is determined by our experience. Exercise helps to enhance and promote our dynamic fitness.

Exercise also helps us to control our weight and improve our body composition by increasing our muscle tissue. This improves the ratio of fat to muscle for our bodies and helps us to sculpt a more ideal body. Studies have shown that exercise is at least equal to and may be even better than dieting in changing this ratio. In addition, exercisers retain more lean muscle tissue whilst dieters lose both fat and lean tissue.

Even more important, exercise has been demonstrated to protect against coronary heart disease (CHD), one of the leading causes of death in this country. Cooper (1982) maintains that aerobic exercise should be of sufficient duration and intensity to have real effects. He recommended that individuals should perform at 70–85 per cent of maximal heart rate non-stop for at least 12 minutes three times per week to improve **cardiovascular system** fitness and significantly reduce the risk for coronary heart disease. The range of target heart rate is computed from a formula based on age and maximum possible heart rate. This has been supported by Lakka *et al.* (1994) in a large-scale five-year study of middle-aged men. Results showed that men with high aerobic fitness were up to 25 per cent less likely to suffer a heart attack compared to those with low aerobic fitness. Increased oxygen use not only provides a workout for the respiratory system (supplying the oxygen) but also for the coronary system (which pumps the blood).

A study of London double-decker bus drivers and their conductors by Morris *et al.* (1953) showed that the more active conductors had significantly less incidence of CHD than did the sedentary drivers. Although other factors may be involved here (in terms of initial selection of people for these jobs for example or bus drivers' being under greater levels of stress than conductors), this study appears to show that workers who are physically active have a reduced risk of coronary heart disease. This finding has since been supported by much larger well-controlled studies. For example, a comprehensive epidemiological study by Paffenbarger *et al.* (1978) of over 17,000 Harvard University graduates dating back to 1916 used detailed activity questionnaires to show that those who were least active after graduation had a 64 per cent increased risk of heart attack compared with their more energetic classmates.

Finally, Brannon and Feist (1997) provide evidence that regular physical exercise affords protection against **stroke** and improves the ratio of high-density lipoproteins (HDL) to low-density lipoproteins (LDL) ('good' and 'bad' cholesterol levels respectively). This in turn reduces the risk of heart disease and protects against some kinds of cancer. Regular physical exercise also prevents bone density loss and helps to control diabetes. It makes you want to go for that jog, doesn't it!

### *Psychological benefits of exercise*

In addition to the above physical benefits of exercise, there are also psychological benefits including decreased depression, reduced anxiety, providing a buffer against stress (Chapter 8) and increasing self-esteem and well-being (through the promotion of positive attitudes, for example).

In the area of depression, people who exercise regularly are generally less depressed than sedentary people are. We do not yet fully understand the mechanisms that protect people who exercise against depression, or the apparent therapeutic effects of exercise for depressed individuals. What we do know is that exercise can lower depressive moods in a variety of people, including young pregnant women from ethnically diverse backgrounds (Koniak-Griffin, 1994) and male and female nursing-home residents aged 66 to 97 (Ruuskanen and Parkatti, 1994). It is also clear that both aerobic and non-aerobic exercise can reduce depression and elevate positive mood states in both normal and clinical populations. Even a brisk walk can make us feel better. These findings could be due in part to the release of endogenous opiates during exercise (e.g. enkephalins and endorphins) which gives us a 'high' in terms of elevated mood.

Exercise also helps reduce state anxiety – a temporary feeling of dread or uneasiness which may arise from a social situation. It is not clear whether exercise can influence trait anxiety (a general feeling of anxiety that is more like a personality characteristic). Studies comparing exercise with relaxation have shown that both techniques are successful in reducing anxiety, although, again, the nature of how this works remains unclear. These techniques could, for example, be creating different states (arousal and relaxation states respectively) or it could simply be that a change in pace is all that is required for reducing anxiety. Other research has shown that combining a change of pace with changes in body composition can be even more effective in reducing anxiety. For example, Norvell and Belles (1993), working with police officers, showed how combining a non-aerobic weight training course with an opportunity to train away from the pressures of work resulted in significant increases in psychological health, including lowered anxiety levels. Similarly, both aerobic and non-aerobic exercise have been used to help people cope with anxiety and even a single session can have positive effects on alleviating depression, fatigue and anger (Pierce and Pate, 1994).

Exercise can also be used as a buffer against stress. This may occur because of the impact of exercise on the immune system. Exercise produces a rise in natural killer cell activity and an increase in the percentage of **T-cells (lymphocytes)** that bear natural killer cell markers (indicating the sites where killer cells are produced). This helps us to ward off potential threats from invading cells before they have the chance to harm the body. One puzzle here is that exercise and stress *both* produce the release of adrenaline and other hormones and yet exercise has a beneficial effect on heart functioning whilst stress may produce lesions in heart tissue. One suggestion here is that, for beneficial effects, adrenaline must be activated and released *infrequently* and *gradually*, under conditions for which it was intended (e.g. jogging) so that it is metabolised differently. In conditions of stress, adrenaline may be discharged in a chronic and enhanced manner, which may be harmful to the body.

Although research suggests that exercise may buffer the effects of stress, the evidence for its effectiveness is mixed. For example, Sinyor *et al.* (1986) failed to find any significant stress buffering benefit for stress in healthy young men who began an aerobic exercise programme or a weight-lifting intervention. In contrast, Roth and Holmes (1985) found that college students who engaged in physical exercise reported fewer stress-related health problems and depressive symptoms than did less active college students. However, this effect disappeared for students who reported low stress to begin with. This indicates that only the combination of high stress and low fitness increases the vulnerability to become sick, suggesting an interaction between stress and fitness on physical and psychological health. Although these studies appear to suggest that the relationship between fitness and stress is complex, it is salutary to note that no study shows that physical activity *lowers* one's resistance to stress.

The benefits of exercise to promoting positive attitudes and enhancing self-image and self-esteem are well known. Sonstroem (1984), in a meta-analysis of the literature (involving a synthesis of many different studies), found a significant positive relationship between exercise and self-esteem. However, many of these studies lacked rigorous experimental design so findings must be treated with caution here. Other uncontrolled factors arising from exercise may have contributed to these findings. However, this absence of reliable evidence should not be taken as evidence of absence of the promising links between exercise and self-esteem. It is at least intuitively correct that people who exercise have more positive feelings about their body shape and physical health and this contributes to feelings of self-esteem. This is supported by research demonstrating a relationship between fitness and self-confidence and self-discipline (Hogan, 1989) and subjective physical health and psychological well-being (Ross and Hayes, 1988).

Finally, a consideration of the effectiveness of exercise for health should also consider its limitations. The main concerns of exercise have focused on the potential dangers of exercise, including the possibility of exercise addiction, injuries arising from exercise and, in rare cases, even death from 'at-risk' individuals who are not closely supervised (Brannon and Feist, 1997). Clearly, effective health gain should take place within a sensible and balanced range of activities, with an awareness of realistic targets and an understanding of bodily responses to exercise.

### Nutrition: diet and health

The contribution of diet to health and ill-health is also well known. Simone (1983) estimated that nutritional factors account for 60 per cent of all cancer in women and 40 per cent of all cancer in men in the USA. Poor dietary practices are associated with cancers of the breast, stomach, uterus, endometrium, rectum, colon, kidneys, small intestine, pancreas, liver, ovary, bladder, prostate, mouth, pharynx, thyroid and oesophagus (Brannon and Feist, 1997).

The main concern here involves eating foods that are high in carcinogens, either as a natural component or as a food additive. The so-called 'natural' foods (i.e. without added chemicals or preservatives) may not necessarily be safer to eat than those containing preservatives and indeed some may be less safe. Recent controversies in the UK involving the chemical spraying of crops and, more recently, the genetic modification of food produce have contributed to this ongoing debate.

Foods that are lacking in preservatives may result in high levels of bacteria and fungi being produced and spoiled food is a risk factor in stomach cancer. Increased education of these dangers, and related developments in food hygiene, have helped produce a sharp decline in this disease. For example, there has been an increased use of food refrigeration in the last 65 years and lower consumption of salt-cured foods, smoked foods and food stored at room temperature (Brannon and Feist, 1997).

The excessive use of salt in the British diet (at both the cooking and the table serving stages) has been linked to hypertension and to cardiovascular disease. In addition, high levels of fats and dietary cholesterol have been tied to atherosclerosis and, ultimately, to coronary heart disease (CHD). A poor diet produces high levels of low-density lipoproteins (LDL: see benefits of exercise, above) and this may aggravate other risk factors for health. The links between fat consumption and breast cancer in women is less clear than for CHD. This is due in part to the different samples of women studied, which has produced mixed findings. Wide cultural variations in fat intake have also further compounded this relationship. However, a large-scale study of Italian and American female breast cancer patients found that these patients *do* show increased fat intake in their diets, although this was due almost entirely to their very high consumption of milk, high-fat cheese and butter. Women who consumed half of their calories as fat had breast cancer rates that were three times higher than average. There were also no differences between these cancer patients and healthy women in their consumption of carbo-hydrates and vegetable fats (Toniolo *et al.*, 1989). Other research has since supported these findings and it appears that we need to examine the *type* of fat consumed together with the age of the person at risk. High intake of *saturated* fats is a known risk factor for the severity of breast cancer in older women but not younger women (Verrault *et al.*, 1988). However, in this same study, both high and low levels of polyunsaturated fats were directly related to the severity of breast cancer of women, suggesting that this relationship is a complex one.

Diet has also been implicated in lung cancer in men. A 24-year longitudinal study in the USA of male Western Electricity workers found that men who consumed high levels of cholesterol in their diet were twice as likely to develop lung cancer compared with men who consumed low levels of cholesterol. The authors conclude by suggesting that this effect could be traced to the dietary cholesterol found in eggs (Shekelle *et al.*, 1991).

Finally, alcohol has been implicated in cancers of the tongue, tonsils, oesophagus, liver and pancreas. Research in Norway found that frequent drinkers were five times more likely to suffer pancreatic cancer compared with non-drinkers (Heuch *et al.*, 1983). Persistent and excessive drinking may also lead to cirrhosis of the liver (which may not be considered surprising since the liver's main function is to detoxify substances like alcohol). This in turn increases the risk of liver cancer although this disease is quite rare since alcoholics usually die of other causes first.

We have so far considered the negative factors of diet on health although there are foods that may protect us against disease and illness. Vitamins A and C, and selenium, are thought to help reduce the risk of developing cancer. Deficiencies in vitamin A may lead to a deterioration in the stomach's protective lining. Similarly, beta-carotene (a form of vitamin A found in vegetables such as carrots and sweet potatoes for example) is a known protector against some types of cancer. Vitamin C (ascorbic acid) helps prevent the formation of nitrosamine carcinogens and appears to have the potential to protect against cancer. Selenium is an important trace element found in grain products and in meat from grain-fed animals. In excess selenium is toxic, but in moderate amounts it may provide some protection against cancer. Care must be taken in interpreting these findings, however, since they are based on reducing relative risks rather than offering complete protection. More research is required to determine the precise relationships between specific nutrients and specific cancer sites in humans.

Research in health psychology also suggests that a high-fibre diet offers protection for both men and women against cancer, although this is mostly limited to colon and rectum cancers. Fibre from fruits and vegetables seems to offer more protection against colon cancer than that from cereals and other grains, although the evidence here is mixed. It is argued that fruit consumption offers even more protection against lung cancer, and that we all should be eating fruit three to seven times per week (Fraser *et al.*, 1991).

## Obesity and eating disorders

**Obesity** is a difficult concept to define for many reasons. Under-standing of obesity varies in terms of personal, social and cultural standards. It is therefore more complex than a measure of an indi-vidual's body-weight. Specifically, obesity is more accurately defined in terms of the percentage and distribution of an individual's body fat, although this again is difficult to assess. Techniques used to assess body fat range from using computer tomography (e.g. ultrasound waves) to magnetic resonance imaging (MRI). Obesity may also be defined in terms of body mass index (BMI) which is calculated by dividing a person's weight (kg) by their height squared $(m^2)$. Stunkard (1984 cited in Ogden, 1996) suggested that obesity should be categorised as either mild (20–40 per cent overweight), moderate (41–100 per cent overweight) or severe (more than 100 per cent overweight). On this basis, research suggests that 24 per cent of American men and 27 per cent of American women are at least mildly obese (Kuczmarski, 1992). Slightly lower estimates are recorded in the UK although both countries report small increases in these estimates in recent years.

Obesity has been associated with both physical health problems (cardiovascular disease, diabetes, joint trauma, cancer, hypertension and mortality) and psychological problems (low self-esteem, poor self-image) although individual differences in response to these make generalisations difficult. Obese people also tend to be attributed causes by others as to how they became obese based on false stereotypes and misinformation, possibly extending back to childhood (Lerner and Gellert, 1969).

Causes of obesity are suggested by physiological theories, metabolic rate theories and behavioural theories (Ogden, 1996). Physiological theories suggest that there is genetic support for obesity running in families (although this is often confounded with the fact that family members usually share similar environments). Metabolic rate theories propose that obese people have a lower resting metabolic rate, burn up less calories when resting and therefore require less food intake. They also tend to have more fat cells, mostly determined by genetic factors. Behavioural theories suggest that obese people tend to be less physically active and have higher food intake than required (not necessarily more than other people). The current view is that only a multidimensional theory can adequately account for obesity. Genetic factors may produce a *predisposition* that results in low activity levels and higher food intake than necessary. Indeed, obesity may not be the result of food intake at all but rather due to medical factors that are outside an individual's personal control.

### Eating disorders

In recent years, there has been a dramatic increase in the incidence of eating disorders, notably in the adolescent female population of Western countries. The two main eating disorders are **anorexia nervosa** and **bulimia** (both of which involve a pathological desire *not* to gain weight).

Anorexia was first discovered by a London doctor, Sir William Gull, in 1874, and is distinguished by an extreme, self-imposed weight loss. Gull regarded the condition as a psychological disorder and coined the term *anorexia nervosa* to indicate a 'loss of appetite through nervous causes' (i.e. psychological factors). With advances in understanding of both psychology and medicine, and based on standards set by the American Psychiatric Association (APA, 1987), individuals are diagnosed as anorexic only if they weigh at least 15 per cent less than their minimal normal weight and have stopped menstruating (cessation of periods). In extreme cases, however, anorexics may weigh less that 50 per cent of their normal weight. The weight loss can lead to a number of potentially dangerous side effects, including emaciation (wasting of the body), susceptibility to infection and other symptoms of undernourishment. Although females are twenty times more likely to develop anorexia than males (particularly amongst white, Western, middle–upper class, teenage women), the incidence of male anorexia appears to be increasing.

Other characteristics of anorexia nervosa include distortions of body image. Anorexics frequently think that they look too fat. Research by Garfinkel and Garner (1982 cited in Atkinson *et al.*, 1993) supported this by comparing the responses of female anorexics with controls on a task involving distortions of body image, as shown in Figure 7.1. Participants used a device that could adjust pictures of themselves and others up to 20 per cent above or below their actual body size, as shown in the figure. An anorexic was far more likely to adjust a picture of herself so that it was larger than their actual size. Interestingly, anorexics did not do the same for photographs of other people, suggesting a distorted body image for themselves only rather than a generalised distortion of body type. These results suggest that anorexics' refusal to eat may be mediated by their image of themselves as too fat (Atkinson *et al.*, 1993).

Further research using male and female undergraduates in the USA suggested that there were gender differences in perception of

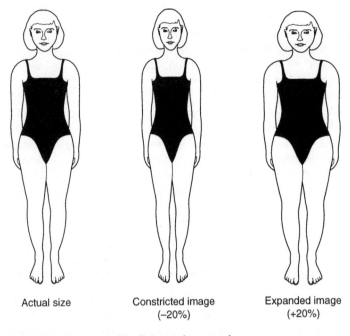

Actual size      Constricted image      Expanded image
(−20%)      (+20%)

*Figure 7.1* **Distortions of body image in anorexics**
*Source*: Adapted from figure originally titled 'Distortions in body image' in
Atkinson *et al.* (1993), after Garfinkel and Garner (1982).

self-body image and ideal body image. Males and females were
shown figures of their own sex and asked to indicate the figure that
looked most like their own shape, their ideal figure and the figure they
felt would be most attractive to the opposite sex. Men selected very
similar figures for all three body shapes! Women on the other
hand selected very different figures for their current figure and either
their ideal figure or the figure they thought would be most attractive
to the opposite sex, as shown in Figure 7.2. Interestingly, when
college males were asked to select the female figure they would
be most attracted to, their average choice was substantially heavier
than college females had selected either as their ideal or as being
most attractive to the opposite sex (Fallon and Rozin, 1985, cited
in Atkinson *et al.*, 1993). This suggests that social norms may be
operating differently for men and women, at least at an American
University. Indeed Logue (1991, cited in Atkinson *et al.*, 1993)

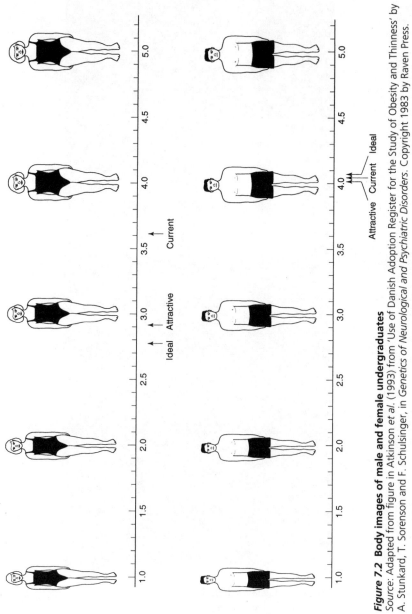

**Figure 7.2 Body images of male and female undergraduates**

Source: Adapted from figure in Atkinson et al. (1993) from 'Use of Danish Adoption Register for the Study of Obesity and Thinness' by A. Stunkard, T. Sorenson and F. Schulsinger, in *Genetics of Neurological and Psychiatric Disorders*. Copyright 1983 by Raven Press.

*Figure 7.3* **Jayne Mansfield**
*Source*: The Kobal Collection

***Figure 7.4*** **Cindy Crawford**
*Source*: The Kobal Collection

suggests that the notion of the 'perfect' figure in women changes over time and place, which in turn influences women's own ideals. Jayne Mansfield was a 'perfect' figure for the 1950s and Cindy Crawford a 'perfect' figure for the 1990s. What will the new millennium bring?

Characteristics of anorexia may help us to understand possible causes and treatments of anorexia (see *Therapeutic Approaches in Psychology* in the Modular Psychology series for more detail here). Such causes are considered to be varied and complex, ranging from genetic factors, through personality factors, to the social–psychological factors suggested above. More recently, there has been increased evidence supporting the view that social norms and psychological factors may trigger a 'potentiality' to acquire anorexia, although the way these factors operate and the nature and direction of causality remain unclear.

Genetic factors suggest a link between anorexia and Turner's syndrome (a disorder in females who lack a second X chromosome) although this relationship is not well established and does not explain anorexia in males. In terms of physiological factors, one possible explanation suggests that the **hypothalamus** (a structure of the forebrain) ceases to function normally. This is further supported by the observation that the hypothalamus controls both eating and hormonal functions (which may also explain irregularities in menstruation). We need to understand more fully how the hypothalamus functions in eating before examining this link further (see *Physiological Basis of Behaviour* in the Modular Psychology series for more detail here).

Psychologists have also been interested in the role of personality factors and family dynamics in anorexia. These may include a lack of self-confidence, need for approval, conscientiousness, perfectionism and the perception of pressure to succeed (Taylor, 1995). Research also suggests that parental psychopathology or alcoholism, or an extremely close or interdependent family, with poor skills for communicating emotion or dealing with conflict, may be pivotal in the development of anorexia (Rakoff, 1983). In particular, the mother–daughter relationship has been implicated in disordered eating. Mothers of anorexic daughters tend to be dissatisfied with their daughter's appearance and tend to be more vulnerable to eating disorders themselves (Pike and Rodin, 1991). More research is required here to explain how the above factors may interact in the onset and development of anorexia.

Finally, treatments for anorexia focus on first bringing the patient's weight back up to a safe level. This is usually achieved within a residential setting. Behavioural techniques based on operant conditioning techniques may be used, rewarding weight gain with social visits for example. However, generalisation of such behaviours may not be easily transferred to the home environment and family therapy may be necessary to help families learn more positive methods of communicating emotion and conflict. Psychotherapy may also be used to improve self-esteem and communication skills, helping the anorexic to cope with stress and manage social pressure.

### *Bulimia*

Bulimia is an eating syndrome characterised by recurrent episodes of binge eating (rapid consumption of a large amount of food in a discrete period of time), followed by attempts to purge the excess eating by means of vomiting and laxatives. Such binges may be frequent and extreme (usually occurring at least once a day, usually in the evening and when alone). Vomiting and use of laxatives can also disrupt the balance of the electrolyte potassium in the body, resulting in dehydration, cardiac arrhythmias (irregular heart-beat) and urinary infections.

Like anorexia, this disorder mainly affects young women although it is more common than anorexia (affecting 5–10 per cent of American women to some degree). Unlike anorexia (which typically affects middle–upper-class females), it also appears to transcend racial, ethnic and socio-economic boundaries. Possible causes for this disorder include biological, personality and social factors, as with anorexia, although the mechanisms involved here are believed to be different.

Bulimics usually suffer from a range of related disorders and experiences, including a history of alcohol or drug abuse, a history of impulsivity and kleptomania (compulsively stealing items that they neither need nor intend to use). It may be triggered by life events, feelings of guilt or depression. Research suggests a stronger link between bulimia and depression compared with anorexia and depression. Depression is relatively common in bulimics (Johnson and Larson, 1982) and both disorders appear to be linked to a deficit in the neurotransmitter substance serotonin. In terms of psychological factors, bulimics may report lacking self-confidence and/or self-identity and using food to fulfil their feelings of longing and emptiness. In the wider social sphere, similar social norms to those discussed above appear to influence bulimics' thinking and behaviour. Binge eating and subsequent vomiting is justified in terms of satisfying the need for a high-calorie intake of food and a desire to stay slim respectively.

Treatment for bulimia involves a combination of medication and cognitive-behavioural therapy matched to suit the individual requirements of the bulimic. The use of anti-depressant drugs has been highly successful with some bulimics although they are not an effective substitute for psychotherapy. Finally, the rationale for successful treatment is more promising for bulimics than for anorexics since bulimics usually do not approve of their own eating habits and are motivated to change their behaviour. This may not necessarily result in their seeking treatment, however, and the challenge here for health practitioners is to provide a supportive framework within which they can seek the treatment they need.

## Summary

In summary, we can see that the kind of lifestyle we lead can significantly impact on our health status, at all stages of the health prevention and promotion cycle. Exercise, fitness and diet all affect how we feel and how we look in addition to the obvious physiological benefits of a healthy lifestyle. In contrast, our increasingly sedentary Western lifestyles and lack of adequate exercise have contributed to a stable increase in the incidence of obesity. Related problems of specific eating disorders have also been shown to have psychological dimensions although the exact mechanisms are difficult to locate. For example, anorexia and bulimia do not have simple causes, characteristics or treatments. This suggests the existence of an interaction of factors at different levels in these often puzzling conditions. Health psychology can make a real contribution to understanding these factors and, more importantly, examining the nature of the relationship within which they operate.

## Further reading

Bennett, P. and Murphy, S. (1997) *Psychology and Health Promotion*, Buckingham: Open University Press. A very good text on health psychology, focusing on health promotion and lifestyle changes using three different approaches: understanding mediators of health and health behaviours (e.g. models of health), facilitating individual change (e.g. targeted interventions) and facilitating population change (e.g. environmental and public policy approaches).

Downie, R. S., Tannahill, C. and Tannahill, A. (1996) *Health Promotion: Models and Values*, Oxford: Oxford University Press. This excellent text reflects the increasing shift in health psychology towards promoting and maintaining health and contains many original concepts and models which future textbooks of health psychology could consider. Wider issues of liberalism, autonomy, values and justice are all considered within a health promotion context.

Ewles, L. and Simnett, I. (1995) *Promoting Health: A Practical Guide*, London: Scutari Press. This text is a very readable, practical guide for understanding and promoting health. There are a range of well-designed activities and exercises in health psychology, for either the individual or the group, which makes learning about health stimulating and enjoyable.

# 8

# Stress and stress management

◆ Nature of stress
◆ Physiology of stress
◆ Coping with stress
◆ Stress management
◆ Stress and illness
◆ Summary

## Nature of stress

**Stress** is an ambiguous term which is used variously to describe the situation, object or person causing stress, the feelings and physical responses elicited in the individual, and the resultant outcomes, whether these are behavioural, cognitive or physiological (Hayward, 1998). It is perhaps useful here to distinguish between **stressors**, **stress responses** and **stress** which this definition refers to. Stressors are the events that an individual perceives as endangering his or her physical or psychological well-being. They may be internal (e.g. pain), external (e.g. changes in the environment such as heat, crowding or noise) or social (e.g. delivering a speech). Stress responses refers to the reactions to such events and may include bodily changes that prepare for emergency (the **fight-or-flight response**) as well as such psychological reactions as anxiety, anger and aggression, apathy and depression, and cognitive impairment. Stress is a state that occurs when people encounter events that they perceive as endangering their physical or psychological well-being. This may result, for example, when an individual feels that the demands placed upon them exceed their perceived ability to deal effectively with them. In summary, stress is a state caused by stressors, resulting in the production of stress responses designed to cope effectively with an unpleasant situation.

Challenges are faced here when one recognises that the relationship between stress and stress responses may be complex. For example, excess heat may be pleasant or unpleasant, depending on whether we are working in a hot workroom or lying on the beach for example. Similarly, there are individual differences in response to stressors, both between individuals and for the same individual across time.

## Physiology of stress

### Role of the nervous system

The basic function of the nervous system is to integrate all the body's systems, using a network of communication to relay information about internal and external conditions to and from the brain. The basic building blocks of the nervous system are **nerve cells** or **neurones**. The actions of each neurone are electrochemical. Inside each neurone, electrically charged ions hold the potential for an electrical discharge. When discharged, a minute electrical current travels the entire length of the neurone. This results in the release of chemicals called neuro-transmitters that are manufactured within each neurone and stored at the end of each neurone. The released **neurotransmitters** diffuse across the synaptic cleft, the space between each neurone. This process continues as the nervous system 'talks' using these electrical and chemical signals.

The basic structure of the nervous system is hierarchical, with major divisions and sub-divisions. The two main divisions of the nervous system are the central nervous system (CNS) and the peripheral nervous system (PNS). The CNS is composed of the brain and spinal cord, and the PNS consists of all other neurones, as illustrated in Figure 8.1.

The peripheral nervous system (lying outside the brain and spinal cord) consists of two parts: the **somatic nervous system** and the **autonomic nervous system**. The somatic nervous system transmits messages arising from stimulation of the skins and muscles to the

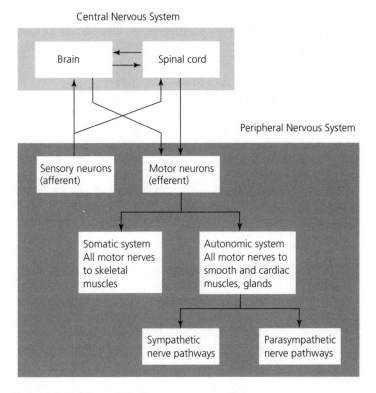

***Figure 8.1*** **Divisions of the human nervous system**

*Source*: From *Health Psychology: An Introduction to Behavior and Health, 3/e, 3rd edition*, by L. Brannon and J. Feist. © 1997. Reprinted with permission of Wadsworth Publishing, a division of International Thomson Publishing. Fax 800 730-2215.

brain using sensory nerves. The autonomic nervous system (ANS) or 'self-governing' system has, at least until recently, been considered outside of conscious or voluntary control. It is the ANS that is mostly involved in the stress response.

The ANS has two main divisions: the **sympathetic nervous system** and the *parasympathetic nervous system*. These two systems are anatomically as well as functionally different, as shown in Figure 8.2.

The sympathetic branch of the ANS mobilises the body's resources in response to an emergency or stressful and emotional

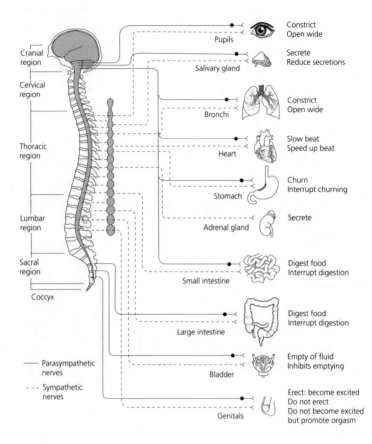

*Figure 8.2* **Autonomic nervous system**

*Source*: Originally titled 'Autonomic nervous system and target organs'. From *Biological Psychology, 2/e, 2nd edition*, by J. Kalat. © 1984. Reprinted with permission of Wadsworth Publishing, a division of International Thomson Publishing. Fax 800 730-2215.

situations. This is often referred to as the 'fight–flight' responses where an organism prepares either to face the stressor or to run away. Either way, the body has to be prepared for motor activity including attack, defence or escape. The events that take place in preparation for this event, as illustrated above, include an increase in heart rate, constriction (narrowing) of blood vessels in the skin, a decrease of gastrointestinal activity, an increase in respiration, stimulation of the sweat glands and dilation of the pupils in the eyes.

The parasympathetic branch of the ANS on the other hand, works to promote relaxation and bring the above functions under stable, normal, non-stressful conditions (e.g. reducing heart rate and respiration etc.). These two systems serve the same target organs (e.g. heart) but function reciprocally. In other words, both systems are operating at the same time, maintaining balance, rather than one being followed by the other. As with other parts of the nervous system, neurones in the ANS are activated by neurotransmitters. The two main neurotransmitters here are acetylcholine and noradrenaline (or norepinephrine). Since each organ has different receptors, these two neurotransmitters have different effects and the relative balance of each is important here in allowing a wide variety of responses.

### Role of the neuroendocrine system

The **endocrine system** is also involved in the stress response and consists of ductless glands. These glands manufacture one or more hormones which they secrete directly into the bloodstream, and which are then distributed throughout the body. The neuroendocrine system consists of those endocrine glands that are controlled by the nervous system. Glands of both systems secrete chemicals known as 'hormones' direct into the bloodstream and these are then carried to different parts of the body.

The endocrine and nervous systems work closely together and share, synthesise and release chemicals. The main difference here is that in the nervous system, these chemicals are called neurotransmitters whilst in the endocrine system they are called hormones. In addition, neurotransmitters are faster acting with short-term effects. Hormones are slower acting (taking minutes or even hours) but longer lasting. The endocrine and nervous systems both have communication and control functions, and both work towards maintaining integrated and adaptive behaviours.

A good example of the interdependency of these two systems is found in the pituitary system. The pituitary gland is connected to the hypothalamus and the two work together to produce and regulate hormones. The pituitary gland is often referred to as the 'master

**127**

gland' because it produces a number of hormones that affect other glands and stimulates the production of other hormones. One of these hormones, adrenocorticotropic hormone (ACTH) plays an essential role in the stress response. Under conditions of stress, the hypothalamus stimulates the pituitary gland to release ACTH, which in turn acts on the **adrenal glands**.

### Adrenal glands

The adrenal glands and endocrine glands are situated on the top of each kidney and each gland comprises an outer covering, the adrenal cortex and an inner covering, the adrenal medulla. Both secrete hormones in response to stress. ACTH from the pituitary stimulates the adrenal cortex to release glucocorticoids (hormone), an example of which is cortisol. This is sometimes referred to as the 'stress hormone' and is used as a physiological index of stress.

The adrenal medulla, activated by the sympathetic nervous system, secretes **catecholamines**. These are a class of chemicals containing adrenaline (or epinephrine) and noradrenaline. Adrenaline is produced only by the adrenal medulla and accounts for about 80 per cent of the total hormone production of the adrenal glands. Noradrenaline is also produced here as well as in many other places in the body.

The physiological response to stress therefore involves the sympathetic division of the ANS interacting with the neuroendocrine system and this in turn interacts with the pituitary and adrenal glands. The chain of events here involves the sympathetic division stimulating the adrenal medulla, which produces catecholamines (adrenaline and noradrenaline). The pituitary releases ACTH, which in turn affects the adrenal cortex.. Glucocorticoid release (e.g. cortisol) prepares the body to release the stress and even cope with the injury. The ANS activation is rapid whilst the actions of the neuroendocrine systems are slower. Together, these systems make up the stress response. For more detail of this process, see *Physiological Basis of Behaviour*, also in this series.

### Theories of stress

So far, we have considered stress from a physiological perspective. However, this explanation is incomplete without a consideration of related psychological factors that accompany this stress response.

Indeed, the real challenge here is to match the language of psychology with the language of physiology by showing how these two overlap and interact with one another. In this way, we can better understand the complex relationship between psychology and physiology, which the biopsychosocial model of health described earlier seeks to explain. In psychological terms, stress may be considered as an environmental stimulus (e.g. Selye, 1956), a response to environmental stimuli (e.g. Selye, 1982) or an interaction of the two (e.g. Lazarus and Folkman, 1984).

### Selye's general adaptation syndrome

Hans Selye conducted much research into stress from the 1930s until he died in 1982; he popularised the term and suggested strong links between stress and physical illness. He initially viewed stress as a stimulus but extended this belief to a response that an organism makes, thus being the first to distinguish the term *stressor* from *stress*. Selye saw stress as a non-specific response that could be caused by any number of environmental stressors. The term 'non-specific' simply meant that the body responded in the same way to stress, regardless of the nature of the stressor(s). In addition to this, Selye proposed a model of how the body mobilised itself for dealing with stress and this became known as the **general adaptation syndrome (GAS)**; it dealt with stress in the following three stages as illustrated in Figure 8.3.

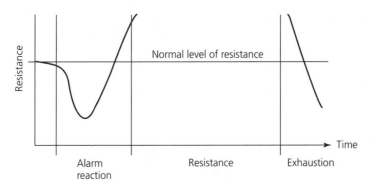

*Figure 8.3* **The general adaptation syndrome**
*Source*: P. Banyard (1996, p. 21) with permission from Hodder & Stoughton Educational.

*Alarm reaction*

This initial response mobilises the body in response to stress by activating the autonomic nervous system (ANS) to prepare for a 'fight-or-flight' response (see physiology of stress, above). Adrenaline is released, heart rate and blood pressure increase, respiration becomes faster and blood is diverted away from the internal organs and towards the skeletal muscles, ready for action. In addition, sweat glands are activated and the gastrointestinal system decreases its activity. In the short term, these responses are highly adaptive, warding off danger as it arises. The problem here is that many modern stress situations may produce long-term exposure to stress for which this response would be inappropriate or even potentially harmful.

*Resistance stage*

In this stage, the organism adapts to the stressor. The duration of adaptation depends on how severe the stressor is and on how adaptive the organism is in coping with the stressor. Greater adaptation here means a longer resistance period, although there are limits in terms of how long the body can cope in this stage. Selye believed that persistent levels of stress produce continued neurological and hormonal changes, which may disrupt the body's internal functioning. This in turn may produce *diseases of adaptation* including peptic (stomach) ulcers and ulcerative colitis (inflammation of the colon), hypertension and cardiovascular disease, hyperthyroidism and bronchial asthma. In addition, Selye believed that these changes may also weaken the immune system, making the risk of infection from other agents more likely.

*Exhaustion stage*

In this stage, the organism's ability to resist is depleted, resulting in a breakdown. The parasympathetic division of the autonomic nervous system is activated, as it normally is to help maintain balance with the sympathetic division. The problem here, however, is that because the sympathetic activity is so abnormally high, the parasympathetic activity is abnormally low to compensate for this. As a result, exhaustion usually results and this may lead to depression or even death.

Selye's GAS remains a fascinating explanation of adjustment to stress although there is an overemphasis on physiological factors here at the expense of psychological factors. In particular, Selye has been criticised for failing to recognise sufficiently the role of emotional and cognitive (i.e. interpretational) factors in stress. Indeed, Mason (1975) argues that it is the emotional dimension that is responsible for the consistency in the stress response.

Selye also used animals to support his research on human responses to stress, which has been criticised for failing to consider extrapolation problems and ignoring uniquely human factors of perception and interpretation in the experience of stress. As a result, Lazarus and Folkman (1984) emphasised the need to include these additional factors in explaining stress in proposing a transactional model of stress.

### Lazarus and Folkman's (1984) transactional model of stress

Lazarus and Folkman believed that the interpretation of the stressful events was more important than the events themselves. It is the perception of potential harm, threats and challenges, together with how confident we are in dealing with these, that determines our ability to cope with stress. Losing a job, for example, may be very stressful for an individual who has no other skills or opportunities to fall back on, whilst it may be only mildly stressful to someone who is already seeking to grow in a different direction. Lazarus and Folkman worked mainly with humans rather than non-human animals in developing their research and theory and this is reflected in their emphasis on the need to consider higher-level cognitive abilities, such as appraisal, in explaining stress. Ironically, Lazarus and Folkman believed that humans were more vulnerable to particular kinds of stress than non-human animals because of the lifestyles we lead and the environments we live in.

Lazarus and Folkman define stress as 'a particular relationship between the person and the environment that is appraised by the person as taxing or exceeding his or her resources and endangering his or her well-being' (1984, p. 19). This represents a *transactional* approach, emphasising the interaction between the person and his or her environment in determining stress. It also emphasises the importance of appraisal in determining the nature of this transaction and considers stress to arise only in situations that are appraised as threatening, challenging or potentially harmful.

Lazarus and Folkman (1984) define three forms of appraisal in dealing with stress.

First, we make a **primary appraisal** of the situation we are in by cognitively appraising the effect of the situation (or stimulus) on our well-being. An event may be appraised as irrelevant, benign–positive or stressful. An irrelevant appraisal will usually have no effect on our emotions; a benign–positive appraisal means the event is seen as having good implications; and a stressful appraisal can mean that the event is seen as harmful, threatening or challenging. In addition, each of these appraisals is likely to generate a different emotion. Lazarus and Folkman defined 'harm' as the psychological damage that has already been done, such as illness or injury for example. 'Threat' was defined as the appraised anticipation of harm and 'challenge' was defined as a person's confidence in overcoming difficult demands. An appraisal of harm may generate anger, disgust, disappointment or sadness; an appraisal of threat may generate worry, anxiety or fear; and an appraisal of challenge may generate anticipation, expectation or excitement. These emotions do not produce stress directly but rather are mediated by the individual's appraisal of an event.

After this appraisal, we then make a **secondary appraisal** of the situation we are in by asking how best can we deal with this situation. Related questions are asked here, including 'what options are available to me?'; 'what is the likelihood that I will be successful in my strategies to reduce distress?'; and 'will this strategy alleviate my distress?'.

Finally, we make a **reappraisal** of our stressful situation and our responses to it by making use of changing information as it becomes available. This emphasises the transactional nature of this model and demonstrates the interaction of the person with their environment over time. Reappraisal may not necessarily reduce stress further. In fact, it may actually increase stress if, for example, a previously benign or irrelevant stimulus is later seen as threatening.

- This model has successfully incorporated the active features of stress and emphasised the need to consider cognitive factors (e.g. perception) in understanding the stress response.
- Several studies have since examined the effect of appraisal on stress and found support for the role of interpretation or appraisal in coping with stress (Ogden, 1996)
- Lazarus and Folkman's (1984) transactional model is descriptive rather than explanatory. Although elegant in design, future research needs to investigate the precise mechanisms (physiological, psychological, etc.) involved in appraisal and consider how or in what ways these processes influence the stress response.

Think back to the last time that you experienced an event that you considered to be a stressful one. Write down how you appraised this event using three columns headed: primary, secondary and reappraisal. Note how your thoughts and feelings changed as your problem was managed. How successful were you in dealing with the problem and what did you learn from this experience?

Progress exercise

## Coping with stress

Lazarus and Folkman (1984) define coping as 'constantly changing cognitive and behavioral efforts to manage specific external and/or internal demands that are appraised as taxing or exceeding the resources of the person' (p. 141). Coping with stress is therefore a process (rather than an event) and something that we learn to do based on our experiences of previously stressful situations. It is also recognised here that coping requires effort to manage the situation the individual is in and that they may not necessarily be aware of their coping responses. Finally, it is useful to recognise that successful coping does not require mastery or perfection. Some things in life are beyond our control and coping is more about management of a situation than solving problems successfully.

There are two main types of coping skills according to Lazarus and Folkman (1984): *problem-focused coping* and *emotion-focused coping*. As its name suggests, the former strategy focuses on dealing with the problem or situation itself, for example, by restructuring the nature of the challenge. Emotion-focused coping is based on dealing with our emotions associated with the situation rather than managing the situation itself. For example, we may use defence mechanisms such as denial or displacement to protect our unpleasant feelings towards the situation. The problem arises here when we adopt an inappropriate coping strategy in relation to the one that is required to effectively manage the stressor (e.g. we may focus too much on a colleague's feelings in a work-based problem for example). These different strategies have resulted in questionnaires being developed that seek to identify different coping styles that individuals use in managing stress. One example is the *Ways of Coping Questionnaire* (Folkman and Lazarus, 1988) which asks individuals to name a specific stressor (e.g. starting college) and then rate how stressful the experience had been on a five-point scale.

There are also individual differences in coping effectiveness depending on our health state or energy levels for example. Individuals who report high levels of *hardiness* (Kobasa, 1979), a personality construct involving *control* (e.g. I can influence events in my life); *commitment* (e.g. I have a sense or purpose and direction in my life); and *challenge* (e.g. I see change as an opportunity rather than as a threat) also report more successful coping strategies. Lazarus and Folkman (1984) also state that effective problem-solving skills, confident social skills, adequate material resources and social support are all important in helping people to manage their stressful situations.

## EVALUATION OF COPING RESEARCH

- The importance of coping strategies has gained general acceptance by health professionals. However, the diversity of coping styles and strategies makes it difficult to identify which techniques are best in aiding recovery (Pitts and Phillips, 1998).
- Individual differences in coping effectiveness (see Kobasa, 1979 above) lead to specific predictions about which specific individuals are most likely to recover from specific illnesses and under what particular conditions.

Think back to your stressful event above. Add detail here in terms of the specific coping strategies that you used. How successful were they? With the benefit of hindsight, what other factors listed above may have helped you to better manage this situation? Can you think of other factors that may also have played a role but which are not listed above?

We have already considered strategies used in *coping* with stress in the Lazarus and Folkman model above. In addition, many of the treatments used in *treating* the effects of stress (e.g. when coping techniques have failed for example) are also used in the treatment of pain. These include the use of medical treatments (e.g. drugs) and psychological treatments (e.g. hypnosis, relaxation training and cognitive-behaviour therapy). See Chapter 4 for a description and review of these interventions.

*Progress exercise*

## Stress management

We saw above that individuals may adopt different coping strategies in response to stress. This is part of the wider area of stress management, which also considers interventions used to combat stress and protect the individual against future episodes of stress in their lives. Stress management may involve the use of biofeedback, behaviour modification, cognitive therapy and exercise. In addition, hypnosis, meditation and relaxation techniques have also been used. All of these have been demonstrated to have benefits in either the management or prevention of stress, and they have been considered in earlier chapters (see Chapter 4 in particular).

### *Stress inoculation*

Finally, the use of stress inoculation (Meichenbaum and Cameron, 1983) has successfully applied similar techniques to those used for the treatment of pain and the management of stress. Stress inoculation includes three stages:

- conceptualisation
- skills acquisition
- rehearsal, and follow-through or application

The conceptualisation stage uses a cognitive interview in which a cognitive therapist works with patients to identify and clarify the nature of their stress. Patients are educated about the nature and effects of stress, and learn about how inoculation works to manage their stress. In the skills acquisition and rehearsal stage, educational and behavioural components are used to enhance patients' repertoire of coping skills: for example, learning new ways of coping with stress. Emphasis is placed on teaching the person self-instruction to change cognitions where necessary. This may involve, for example, patients' learning to 'self-talk', monitoring their own internal dialogue and changing negative thoughts where required. In the application and follow-through stage, patients put into practice the cognitive changes they achieved in the two previous stages.

### EVALUATION OF STRESS INOCULATION TECHNIQUES

Stress inoculation has been effective in a variety of stressful situations, ranging from anxiety about mathematics in college students, managing hypertension in all age groups and stress management in general. It has also been successfully combined with other treatment methods discussed above to alleviate stress. For example, Kiselica *et al.* (1994) used a combination of stress inoculation, progressive muscle relaxation, cognitive restructuring and assertiveness training to significantly reduce trait-anxiety and stress-related symptoms among adolescents. These results, however, did not extend to their improving academic performance, suggesting that other factors may also be involved here. Although most evidence reviewing inoculation training suggests only positive effects in terms of stress management, there remains a lack of understanding of the mechanisms through which this technique works and such interventions cannot necessarily rule out the possibility of placebo or expectancy effects also contributing to these findings.

## Stress and illness

The relationship between stress and illness is a complex one. As we have seen, illness and disease may be caused by many factors including genetic factors, biological factors, psychological factors, lifestyle and even our social environment. It is perhaps not surprising therefore that studies correlating stress with illness have found only small correlations between the two (usually not exceeding 0.20).

Stress has, however, been linked with a range of physical illnesses including headaches, infectious illness (e.g. influenza), cardiovascular disease, diabetes, asthma and rheumatoid arthritis. In addition, stress shows some relationship to negative moods and mood disorders such as depression and anxiety disorders (Brannon and Feist, 1997).

The main problem in demonstrating the links between stress and illness lies with identifying the physiological or psychological pathways that mediate or connect the two. This may occur directly through effects on the nervous system and endocrine system or on the immune system. All of these systems have the potential to create physical illness so there is a strong basis for physiological links here. More research is required, however, in terms of examining which specific pathways mediate specific types of illness in response to activation by specific stressors. In addition, indirect effects could occur through changes in health practices that increase risks for illness. For example, engaging in risky behaviours (e.g. substance abuse) may lead indirectly to disease or illness using similar pathways.

### The role of the immune system in stress

We saw from Selye's model above that one of the consequences of stress was suppression of the immune system. We now know that there are complex interactions between the nervous, endocrine and immune systems in response to stress and the result of this has been implicated in the above disorders. The immune system, like the endocrine system and the nervous system, is distributed throughout the body. Leucocytes (white blood cells) form the basis of the cell population in the immune system and these are differentiated into many different types, each with a specific function, but all with the same aim of repelling the body's invaders (Hayward, 1998).

Some of these cells are manufactured in the bone marrow of the long bones, whilst others (T-cells) mature in the thymus gland. There are also groups (nodes) of cells associated with the immune system, and these are located in the lymph system. Cells circulate in the lymph fluid and in the bloodstream. High levels of white blood cells may not always be a sign of a healthy immune system since they may not be producing a targeted response to an infection.

Recent research by Evans *et al.* (1997) into psychoneuro-immunology (PNI), which looks at the influence of psychology on the nervous and immune systems, has found the assumption that stress suppresses the immune system to be oversimplified. Evans *et al.* have suggested that individual measures of the state of the immune system during stress may vary with the type of stress, its duration and even its timing. Instead of talking about enhanced and suppressed immunity, therefore, it is more useful to see the immune system to be constantly striving for a state of balance (or 'homeostasis'). The different systems above are constantly responding with 'up-regulation' and 'down-regulation' (i.e. raised and lowered capacity of lymphocyte cells fighting invading bacteria or viruses).

## Summary

We have seen that stress and stress management is a potentially complex topic, with many factors to consider in understanding the stress experience and response. Stress involves physiological (e.g. immune, endocrine, neural) and psychological factors, and the challenge now is to make further links between these. Coping with stress and treating stress are both influenced by our beliefs about the causes of stress, and research suggests that stress is not a unitary concept, although our physiological response to it may show sufficient predictability to make successful protection and interventions increasingly more effective (e.g. inoculation techniques).

## Further reading

Cooper, C. L. (1996) *Handbook of Stress, Medicine and Health*, London: CRC Press.

Fisher, S. and Reason, J. (1989) *Handbook of Life Stress, Cognition, and Health*, Chichester: Wiley.

The above two texts are both edited collections on stress and published as 'handbooks' of stress.

Evans, P., Clow, A. and Hucklebridge, F. (1997) 'Stress and the immune system', *The Psychologist* 10(7), 303–7. A very interesting article on the (increasingly researched) relationship between stress and the immune system.

Lazarus, R. S. and Folkman, S. (1984) *Stress, Appraisal and Coping*,

New York: Springer. A classic textbook on stress and coping responses.

Silber, K. (1999) *The Physiology of Behaviour*, London: Routledge. This text provides comprehensive coverage of the physiological basis of stress and the stress response.

# 9

# Study aids

## IMPROVING YOUR ESSAY WRITING SKILLS

At this point in the book you have acquired the knowledge necessary to tackle the exam itself. Answering exam questions is a skill that this chapter shows you how to improve. Examiners are able to use their experience of marking exam scripts to show you what to aim for and what to avoid doing in examinations. In particular, there are two main reasons why students may not perform well in exams. The first lies in a failure to answer the specific question(s) set. For example, when asked to write about why patients may not comply (adhere) to medical requests, some students may write about the effectiveness of certain treatments for certain conditions, without any reference to the notion of compliance (adherence)! Even if their answer is well written, it will receive little or no credit if it does not tackle the question set. The second reason why students may not perform well is that they fail to analyse or evaluate a theory or model or psychological study when asked to do so. Instead, these students tend to describe what they were requested to evaluate. In other words, students do not answer the question in the *way* the examiner wants.

It is often a useful exercise to find out exactly what kind of answer earns what kind of grade. For example, a typical grade C answer is usually accurate but has limited detail and commentary. It is also usually reasonably constructed. To raise such an answer to a grade A or B may require no more than fuller detail, better use of material and a coherent organisation. By studying the student answers presented in this chapter, and the examiner's comments, you can learn how to turn grade C answers into grade A.

The structured answers here are about the length a student would be able to write in 45–50 minutes (leaving you time for planning and checking). Each answer (or part answer) is followed by detailed comments about its strengths and weaknesses. The most common problems to look out for are:

- Failure to answer the specific question asked, as illustrated above.
- Putting the wrong bits in the wrong parts of the question. For example, part (a) asks you to show knowledge and understanding (i.e. what you know and what it means); part (b) asks for evaluation (i.e. what is the quality of the evidence in part (a)); and part (c) asks you to apply the knowledge. What could be simpler?
- Writing 'everything you know' in the hope that something will get credit. Excellence is displayed through selectivity, and therefore carefully selecting material in your answer (and thus rejecting other material not relevant to the set question) can often make improvements.

Below are detailed psychology exam questions, student answers and examiner's commentary from the 1998 OCR paper.

## Practice essay 1

A healthy approach to examinations

Most charities want you to examine your conscience. We'd rather you examined your testicles.

Testicular cancer is the most common cancer in men aged 20–35, with over 1,000 new cases a year. Nowadays 9 out of 10 cases can be cured and it is far better to pick the cancer up early. Whatever your age you should examine your testicles regularly.

Cancer Research Campaign

**(a) Describe what psychologists have discovered about promoting health with regard to a specific problem (e.g. cancer or smoking). (8 marks)**

### Candidate's answer

Psychologists have conducted many studies into health promotion and the differences in approach. Health promotion is any behaviour that helps, enhances or maintains our health. One of these approaches is Janis who conducted a study into whether arousing fear in people influenced them to change or improve a health behaviour. She constructed three lectures on the effects of tooth decay and oral hygiene, each were designed to create a different level of fear. Talk one was minimum-fear; one-third of the subjects who were university students listened to this talk. The next group listened to a talk, which aroused moderate fear and the third group, a talk that aroused high fear where they were shown extreme cases of tooth decay. Janis found that although the third talk aroused the most fear and interest, it also had the highest negative ratings. Janis showed that the group with the least amount of fear showed the highest level of conformity in oral hygiene.

Another approach was the Yale model of communication, which looked at the way in which we need to deliver a message in order to be effective. The Yale model of communication suggested five ways that affect the likelihood of, for example, health promotion being successful.

1 Source – The source needs to be credible i.e. in the case of tooth decay, the ideal source would be a knowledgeable person such as a dentist.
2 Message – The promotion would need to consider whether the audience was sympathetic to a particular illness. If so, then a one sided agreement is more effective. If however the audience is unlikely to be sympathetic about an illness or condition, then both sides of the agreement should be presented. For example, people may not be sympathetic to the condition of tooth decay as they may see it as an individual's fault. In this case, a two-sided argument may be more effective.
3 Medium – How will you spread the message? Flay suggested that the media is the most successful way as it reaches mass audiences.
4 Situation – If an audience is knowledgeable on the situation, the most effective way is to let them draw their own conclusions. However, if an audience is not knowledgeable, then you should state your conclusions.

5 Target – Who the promotion should be aimed at. For example, oral hygiene would be more effective if it was targeted on children in order for them to gain good oral hygiene habits early and prevent decay.

Another point is whether or not people feel threatened enough to act. The Health Belief Model (Rosenstock) suggested that we will only carry out a health behaviour if we perceive the threat as real and even then we need some cue for action. And whether the barriers these might be financial, social etc. are outweighed by the gains – these might be relief from physical symptoms, free from anxiety etc. He's suggested that only then will we act.

Prochaska put forward a five-stage model of behaviour change, which he suggested would influence whether an individual changed their behaviour. He believed that firstly we experience pre-contemplation – no problem recognised, no need for change. Contemplation – realise problem. Preparation – Prepare to change. Action – Change behaviour. Maintenance – maintaining a behaviour e.g. brushing teeth twice a day or not eating sweets for at least six months.

He suggested that individuals may attempt to change behaviour 3–4 times before they reach the maintenance stage.

### Examiner's comments

This part of the question is answered competently, although rather 'rote/list' in approach and does not always consistently focus on the ONE specific problem requested. The candidate has correctly identified and detailed three appropriate approaches, the Yale Model, the Heath Belief Model and the Stages of Change model. The answer could, however, be more focused on health PROMOTION rather than simply on behaviour CHANGE, the latter of which was required in the question. However, the candidate here has provided a good answer and would probably earn a grade A.

**(b) Evaluate what psychologists have discovered about promoting health with regard to a specific problem. (10 marks)**
[Hint: you may want to include points about the effectiveness of promotions, the assumptions about human nature, the ethics of some strategies and the methodology used by psychologists.]

My first evaluation issue is Ethnocentrism. This is concerned with how relevant the study is to other cultures. Whether the study is based on purely white Western ideas and concepts about health promotion. Firstly, the Yale model of communication is ethnocentric in that it only considers Western means of delivering a successful message. It fails to take into account the possibility that other cultures may not have the means of media (Flay) and could not reach mass audiences. The Behavioural Change Model is also ethnocentric in that it looks at change as an individual's choice of action, again Western ideas of individuality which may be irrelevant to more collective societies that see themselves as part of a group. In comparison, the study on fear arousal by Janis could be seen as less ethnocentric as it used a natural human response – fear – and so could be used in other cultures.

My next evaluation issue is reductionism. Whether the study takes a reduced view of a behaviour failing to take into account other factors, which may affect that behaviour. Janis' study into fear arousal was reductionist in that it only took the view that we will act on health if we are scared into doing so, which ignores the fact that social factors may come into play such as Fishbein's reasoned action – the likelihood of behaviour relies on two things: whether it's beneficial and whether it's socially desirable. In comparison, the Yale model of communication takes into account a wider variety of factors such as who's delivering the message, who it's aimed at, how much they know about it etc.

My next evaluation issue is Effectiveness – How effective the study was in promoting health behaviour. Janis' study which looked at fear arousal – she found that fear arousal was not effective or as effective as a lecture without fear in promoting oral hygiene. Despite this fear, arousal campaigns are still widely used in campaigns today. In comparison, the Yale model of communication was formed as a result of studies into what makes a successful message. Therefore it could be said that it would be more effective in promoting health, as it considers social aspects such as who the targets are. In circumstances where the target population are, for example, children, fear arousal may not be an appropriate method of promoting health, so ineffective.

My final evaluation issue is generalisation – can the study be ready generalised to other people (e.g. sub-cultures, different ethnicity, children, older people etc.). Janis conducted her research on students who, because firstly their age, and secondly their knowledge cannot be generalised to non-educated, non-students. For example, older people may experience first hand tooth decay and be more eager to change their health behaviour – as the threat is more realised. The fact that the students were at University meant that they may have been knowledgeable on the subject and realised that extreme cases of tooth decay were rare and unlikely to happen to them. In comparison, the Yale model of communication takes into consideration a wide variety of factors which affect whether a health promotion message will be successful or not, so their findings can be more readily applied.

### Examiner's comments

Again, this is a competent answer which addresses the set question, although it is again presented in a rote/list form (although less so than part (a)) and largely engages explicitly with the set question. The points of evaluation given could be tied more specifically to promoting health with regard to a specific problem. The selected issue of dental hygiene is not considered or applied until the student is half-way through the answer. This should be identified at the start of the answer and then referred to consistently in the subsequent evaluation. In addition, the examiner has suggested wider issues of effectiveness of promotions (suggesting measurement and validity problems etc.), assumptions about human nature (encouraging the general criticisms that most models of behaviour change assume that humans are rational decision makers etc.) and ethical issues of some strategies (e.g. informed consent, protection from harm etc.). The candidate does not consider these. The last area identified in the question hints, methodology, is identified and evaluated effectively although this could be tied explicitly to a selected problem. More specific and explicit information would be useful here which could be obtained by reading, and understanding, a wider range of health psychology research. The mark awarded here would be equivalent to a grade A.

**(c) Outline the main features of a school health promotion programme aimed at EITHER promoting self-examination OR preventing those at school from starting to smoke. (6 marks)**

*Candidate's answer*

In order for a school promotion campaign on preventing substance abuse to be successful, it would have to provide the children with information about, for instance, tobacco. This gives them informational control which reduces the chances of them abusing that substance. They would also need to be given social support which would raise self-efficacy – the feeling of how capable you are of achieving, your general feeling of self worth and value. This could mean that you feel that, for instance, you were capable of saying no to others who offer you substances. The communication would be clear and taking into account the Yale model of communication would involve, for instance, a person suffering from cancer due to smoking – someone who is knowledgeable giving a talk on the effects of smoking.

*Examiner's comments*

This answer is very good, although it does not expand relevant ideas in a way that demonstrates good understanding of the issues involved. Information control is cited here, although the candidate doesn't really explain what it is or how it may reduce the likelihood of abuse. Social support and self-efficacy are used together here implying that the former promotes the latter. The candidate would strengthen this link by simply citing evidence in support (e.g. Bandura, 1977) and/or briefly describing other techniques that might promote self-efficacy in this context. The candidate demonstrates that they understand the concept of self-efficacy applied to this context which is promising. The Yale model of communication is also mentioned although it needs further expansion. For example, this model does not only emphasise knowledge aspects in successful communication but also the source of the message, characteristics of the message itself (e.g. one sided v two sided arguments), the context in which the message is delivered (e.g. lab. v. field) and the characteristics of the receiver(s). Even if some of these features are briefly outlined, this could well raise this part of the answer even higher. Note also here, that evaluation is not required for this part of the question. Finally, notice that the question is focused on prevention in smoking (e.g. rather than treatment) and so more could be made of this earlier stage (e.g. Stages of Change Model). This answer would probably still receive the equivalent of a Grade A.

## Practice essay 2

A spoonful of sugar helps the medicine go down

How widespread is the problem of non-compliance to medical requests?

- The average adherence rate for taking medicine to treat acute illnesses with short-term treatment regimens is about 78%; for chronic illnesses with long-term regimens the rate drops to about 54%.
- The average adherence rates for taking medicine to prevent illness is roughly 60% for both short-term and long-term regimens (treatment programmes).
- Patient's adherence to scheduled appointments with a practitioner is much higher if the patients initiated the appointment than if the practitioner did.
- Adherence to recommended changes in lifestyle, such as stopping smoking or altering one's diet, is generally quite variable and often very low.

[Sarafino (1994) *Health Psychology: Biopsychosocial Interactions*, Wiley, p. 309]

### (a) Describe how psychologists explain why people do not adhere to medical requests. (8 marks)

#### Candidate's answer

Psychologists have done research into why people do not adhere to medical requests. One study was done to show how understanding of medical language affects why people do not comply. Patients attending a surgery were given lists of medical words and asked to remember them. The subjects were split into two groups. One group were given a list containing random medical words (e.g. diseases) and the other group were given a structured and organised list. The findings were that 25% more of the patients could recall the lists that were structured and organised. The lists were also given to medical students (who were familiar to the medical words). The result was 50% more of the students recalled more of the words when the lists were organised.

Another similar study was done but this time the questions were about their personal reports. The results showed that the participants remembered the first things that were said. There was no improvement of recall of the unstructured questions. This evidence implies that communication affects compliance to medical requests. There was an increase in recall when the patients understood some medical knowledge. This suggests that Craik and Lockhart's memory model is correct as the more they understood what was relevant to themselves the more they remembered.

Another study was conducted testing the understanding of medical terms. Several women of low SES (socio-economic status) during their stay in a maternity ward were asked if they knew what 13 medical terms actually meant. The results were that 39% of the women actually knew what the medical terms meant. This was a higher result than the doctors had originally predicted. This suggested that people actually do not comply with medical requests because they do not understand what is being asked of them.

**Locus of control** is also another factor affecting compliance. Studies have been conducted that have shown that people that have an external locus of control comply less than those who have an internal locus of control when, for example, stopping smoking has been recommended. This is because people with an external locus of control have no confidence in themselves and believe that they have no control so they cannot give it up. People with an internal locus of control believe they have the ability to cope with the situation. This shows that personality and locus of control affects level of compliance.

### Examiner's comments

This is a good answer which is directly focused on the set question, wide ranging in coverage, with good description and understanding of factors affecting compliance. It would be useful if the student could cite specific studies in more detail (names/dates of research) although this is less important than accurate and relevant detail. Note that a grade A answer might actively engage with each cited example of non-compliance in the exam question (see above bullet points here) although this is not essential for a grade A. Always be aware that examiner hints and examples are there to help you gain additional marks! This answer would probably score a solid grade B because of its good breadth and understanding.

## (b) Evaluate how psychologists explain non-adherence to medical requests. (10 marks)

[Hint: in your evaluation you may wish to include points about the value of the evidence, the ethics involved in gaining evidence, the difficulties involved in generalising from such research, and the implications for both patients and practitioners.]

### Candidate's answer

One evaluative issue is reductionism. The study of locus of control is reductionist as it identifies only internal factors e.g. personality as the factor that determines the level of compliance. It ignores external factors such as peers. With regard to giving up smoking, it might be that a person has an internal locus of control but does not believe they can deal with giving up smoking as their peers say that they should not give up smoking.

Another issue is ecological validity (how applicable it is to real life). The study conducted at the surgery is high in ecological validity as it is being conducted where the people were already. The patients were not taken to a laboratory and the students would have been in their natural environment.

In comparison, the study about the women in the maternity ward is both high and low in ecological validity. It is high because the participants were already there and not asked to go anywhere drastically different. It is also lacking in ecological validity because women in a maternity ward are not usually asked to complete questionnaires and asked how well they understand medical terms.

This also leads onto the issue of ethics. It can be seen as unethical to ask women questions about their understanding of medical terms whilst they are pregnant and about giving birth. If they scored lowly, then it could lead them to feeling stressed and worried. In the study there is no mention of debriefing to explain that if they obtained a low score that they should not worry. In comparison, none of the studies mention debriefing which is breaking ethical guidelines. The two studies conducted at the surgeries could also lead to the participants feeling stressed if they score poorly. This is a breach of ethical guidelines as the participant is supposed to return from the experiment in the same state as they entered it.

Generaliseability is another issue. The study at the maternity ward had a sample of women with a low SES. This means it cannot be generalised to men, children or those with a higher SES. This questions the studies validity as it cannot be used to explain why others do not adhere to medical requests.

*Examiner's comments*

Again, this part is competently answered, showing some understanding of what is required here in terms of evaluation, although it is rather 'rote' and 'list-centred' without really engaging with these terms. The studies described in part (a) are revisited (which is perfectly acceptable) although the specific details of these studies commented on above remain elusive here. The student uses the issue of ecological validity skilfully here, showing that it can be a strength and a weakness in the same study, depending on what is being assessed. Implications of these findings, for both patients and practitioners, could be discussed here (as suggested) and even common sense arguments might well have promoted this answer to a higher grade. Overall a grade B/C answer.

**(c) Suggest a number of ways in which adherence to medical requests may be improved. (6 marks)**

*Candidate's answer*

In order to improve adherence to medical requests, there are several things that could be done. In people's places of work, they could offer schemes to help people cope with their medical needs. For example, they could give their employees extra pay if they for example give up smoking or go on a diet. They could also lessen people's stress to get back to work as soon as possible. The workplace could give them sufficient time off to recover as long as they did what the doctor told them and took the specified medicine etc.

Operant conditioning is another way to try and improve medical compliance. This could be done using a reward and punishment system. For example, a study was conducted on a girl who was badly burned. To start with, she would not let her wounds be treated. Whenever she was good and let her bandages be administered, she would be given a reward but whenever she cried and refused treatment she would receive nothing. The conditioning helped her to comply with the medical advice. If people are offered an incentive to comply, then this could improve medical compliance.

Better communication is another way to improve compliance. If the doctors do not use medical 'jargon' and make sure the patients understand what they have been told this should improve compliance. Also if the doctors give their patients support, then this could help them to cope with the medical requests e.g. giving up smoking. This support would be most helpful during the action stage of Melzack's Spiral Model as it would help people cope and continue to e.g. giving up smoking or being on a diet.

### Examiner's comments

This is a reasonable although limited answer that uses a combination of basic psychology and common sense to construct advice for improving compliance. The use of operant conditioning (paragraph 2) shows reasonable understanding of the underlying mechanisms of this learning process. Melzack's spiral model appears mis-quoted (no marks lost here however because of positive marking). This should be attributed to Prochaska and DiClemente (1982). In any event, it is not described in sufficient detail to suggest that the student understands this model. This answer would probably receive the equivalent of a grade C here. To lift this answer to a grade A, the student could revisit some of their more considered examples in sections (a) and (b) and apply them to improving compliance more fully. It is often strategy and technique which allows us to do well in exams, applying knowledge and understanding fully to the set question, not sheer genius or luck!

**Practice essay 3**

A little scratch

'This won't hurt a bit', says the doctor just before inflicting excruciating pain on you. How does the doctor know how much pain you will feel? How do psychologists assess or measure pain? Below is an extract from the McGill Pain Questionnaire.

---

Some of the words below describe your *present* pain. Circle *ONLY* those words that best describe it. Leave out any category that is not suitable. Use only a single word in each appropriate category – the one that applies best.

| 1 | 2 | 3 | 4 |
|---|---|---|---|
| Flickering | Jumping | Pricking | Sharp |
| Quivering | Flashing | Boring | Cutting |
| Pulsing | Shooting | Drilling | Lacerating |
| Throbbing | | Stabbing | |
| Beating | | Lancinating | |
| Pounding | | | |

| 5 | 6 | 7 | 8 |
|---|---|---|---|
| Pinching | Tugging | Hot | Tingling |
| Pressing | Pulling | Burning | Itchy |
| Gnawing | Wrenching | Scalding | Smarting |
| Cramping | | Searing | Stinging |
| Crushing | | | |

| 9 | 10 | 11 | 12 |
|---|---|---|---|
| Dull | Tender | Tiring | Sickening |
| Sore | Taut | Exhausting | Suffocating |
| Hurting | Rasping | | |
| Aching | Splitting | | |
| Heavy | | | |

| 13 | 14 | 15 | 16 |
|---|---|---|---|
| Fearful | Punishing | Wretched | Annoying |
| Frightful | Gruelling | Blinding | Troublesome |
| Terrifying | Cruel | | Miserable |
| | Vicious | | Intense |
| | Killing | | Unbearable |

| 17 | 18 | 19 | 20 |
|---|---|---|---|
| Spreading | Tight | Cool | Nagging |
| Radiating | Numb | Cold | Nauseating |
| Penetrating | Drawing | Freezing | Agonizing |
| Piercing | Squeezing | | Dreadful |
| | Tearing | | Torturing |

---

[Reprinted from Banyard (1996) *Applying Psychology to Health*, London: Hodder & Stoughton, p. 163]

**(a) Describe attempts by psychologists to assess or measure pain. (8 marks)**

*Candidate's answer*

For psychologists to measure pain effectively, they need to take a biopsychosocial approach. This means looking at the biological, psychological and social sides of pain. One way of measuring pain is to use self-report measures. You can use a McGill Pain Questionnaire which has different sections and different ways to describe your pain. It asks you where your pain is and if it's internal or external. It asks you what your pain feels like, and it asks you how you feel about your pain. A simpler version of this is to use a rating scale and rate your pain from 1 to 10. Scales for children are used where they are asked to choose a different colour for different types of pain. Then they can colour in a picture of their body showing where they are in most pain.

To measure your pain biologically, you can use machines which measure your nerve activity, called an ecometergraph. Another way to measure pain is to interview the person experiencing the pain on a regular basis. That way you are able to find out a lot about the pain. Also talking to the family of the person in pain helps. You can train their family to notice things they do when they are in a lot of pain e.g. sleep a lot or fidget around all the time. Then the family can note down when they do these things. All things like this help the doctors get a much better all round picture of the person's pain.

*Examiner's comments*

This is a competent answer which addresses the set question rather than giving a general 'everything I know about pain' response. The student therefore demonstrates the skill of selectivity in terms of the information supplied. The answer is accurate, reasonably well detailed and reflects the plurality in the set question (i.e. attempts) which is normally taken to read 'two or more attempts' in this context. The biopsychosocial model applied to pain provides a very useful structure here for describing different measurement techniques (i.e. biological, psychological and social dimensions of pain and its measurement) which is welcomed. However, to promote this answer to a grade A, the McGill Pain Questionnaire (MPQ) could be described in a little more detail. For example, outlining the four parts of MPQ, pain patients mark where they feel most pain using front and back drawings of the human body. They also circle pain descriptors as above, record changes in pain over time and assess intensity of pain on a 5-point scale, ranging from mild to excruciating! The ecometergraph is probably referring to electromyography (EMG) which records the level of muscle tension in patients who suffer from low back pain. Look back at the student's answer here to see that the description here is rather basic and imprecise. Other biological measures not included here include autonomic indices (e.g. measurement of involuntary processes such as blood flow, heart rate and hand surface temperature). Interviews and observations by significant others are also briefly described and this attracts some credit, although again needs more detail (and possibly cited research?) to lift the answer to a grade A. As it stands, this answer would probably earn a high grade C/low grade B.

## (b) Evaluate attempts by psychologists to assess or measure pain. (10 marks)

[Hint: you may wish to consider the following: comparing and contrasting different approaches, assessing the validity and reliability of the measures, individual differences and the usefulness of the measures.]

### *Candidate's answer*

It is unethical to ask the family of the person who is in pain to watch how they behave and note down what they do. This gives the person no privacy. They might be OK but just a bit fidgety and their family may see this that they are in pain.

The McGill Pain Questionnaire is ethnocentric. Other cultures might use different words to describe their pain. You can only use it if you speak and read English so it is not suitable for other cultures and foreign people. It is also not suitable for children who can't yet read and write and don't yet understand what the words mean.

Each of these methods of measuring pain is only good if it is used with the other types. The biological method on its own is no good. We already know they are in pain. The pain questionnaire, especially McGill, is good as they have a wide choice of words and ways to describe your pain. However, it is often hard to think about one word to describe your pain. That's why interviews with the doctor are important to find out how they feel about being ill and how they are coping with it.

## Examiner's comments

Note here that 10 marks are awarded (compared with 8 above) and students are asked to demonstrate skills of evaluation in their answer. The student is struggling a bit here, producing reasonable methodological and procedural criticisms although these lack detailed expansion in terms of the set question. The hints offered here invite the promotion of eclectic (wide ranging synthesis) approaches in measuring pain and the real emphasis here is on the reliability and validity of pain measures (i.e. do the pain measures produce consistent measures and do these measures really measure the pain experience?). In terms of the latter, for example, Andrasik et al. (1982) found no differences between patients with headache pain and patients without headache pain on the above autonomic measures, casting doubt on the validity of these measures. The above answer cites an advantage and disadvantage of the MPQ, which is good, although the degree of analysis is slightly limited here. This answer would probably attract a low grade C.

## (c) Suggest a psychological strategy for reducing pain. Explain the theory on which your suggestion is based. (6 marks)

## Candidate's answer

There are many different psychological strategies for reducing pain. One of these strategies is to use distraction techniques. This is when the patient focuses on a non-painful stimulus in the room. This takes their mind off the pain. A study has been done which shows you can distract yourself by doing things like counting ceiling tiles, singing, listening to someone's voice, listening to music, playing video games etc.

Other psychological strategies that can be used for reducing pain are relaxation and meditation techniques. By doing meditation, like distraction, you are taking your mind off the pain you are in by focusing it on something else. The more you are able to take your mind off the pain the better, and this is most easily done when you have something else to think about.

### *Examiner's comments*

This answer asks for only ONE strategy for reducing pain and the student offers two (or possibly three!). In such cases, examiners usually mark all answers but credit ONLY the best one. The student would have done well to select ONE psychological strategy and focus on elaborating on this here. For the above, however, both answers are similar in terms of demonstrating a rather basic level of descriptive detail and understanding. As a result, this answer would probably be a borderline fail/pass here (fail/grade N).

Hopefully, this experience shows the importance of answering the specific question set, identifying the action words (e.g. describe, evaluate etc.) and ensuring sufficient detail to fully answer the question. With practice and feedback, you are now destined for exam success. Go for it!

# Glossary

The first occurrence of each of these terms is highlighted in **bold** type in the main text.

**A-beta fibre (cutaneous)** Myelinated nerve fibres that respond to mechanical stimuli such as light, pressure or vibration.

**A-delta fibre (cutaneous)** Myelinated nerve fibres that may be stimulated by pressure, heat, cooling or chemicals.

**acupuncture** Therapeutic technique for treating certain painful (and other) conditions by stimulating specific areas of the body surface (e.g. by inserting long thin needles through the skin and stimulating cutaneous nerve fibres).

**acute (pain/stress/disorders)** Illnesses or disorders that occur over a short period of time. They are usually curable.

**adherence** Degree to which an individual follows recommended advice or treatment in response to a health- or illness-related condition.

**adrenal glands** Two small glands, located on top of the kidneys; they are part of the endocrine system that responds to stress.

**adrenaline** A hormone closely related to noradrenaline. Increases heart rate and increases rate and depth of breathing. Also implicated in the modification of pain in response to noxious stimuli.

**aerobic exercise** High-intensity, long-endurance exercise, which is believed to contribute to cardiovascular fitness and other health outcomes.

**afferent** Nerve impulses flowing into the central nervous system; consciously perceived afferent information is described as 'sensory'. Afferent neurones are also referred to as sensory neurones.

**AIDS (acquired immune deficiency syndrome)** Progressive impairment of the immune system caused by the human immuno-deficiency virus (HIV).

**anorexia nervosa** A condition produced by excessive dieting and exercise, resulting in body weight that is grossly below optimal level. It is most commonly found in adolescent girls.

**atherosclerosis** A major cause of heart disease, caused by the narrowing of the arterial walls (e.g. formation of plaques or deposits which reduce blood flow).

**autonomic nervous system (ANS)** That part of the nervous system that controls the activities of the **visceral organs**, and typically cannot be controlled.

**biofeedback** Methods used to provide feedback about the operation of bodily processes (e.g. heart rate), allowing subsequent control of behaviour.

**biomedical model** The viewpoint that illness can be explained in terms of physical (somatic) factors, rather than psychological or social processes. It has been the dominant model in medical practice until recently.

**biopsychosocial model** The view that biological, psychological and social factors are all involved in any given state of health or illness.

**blood pressure** The force that blood exerts against vessel walls.

**breast self-examination (BSE)** Monthly practice of checking the breasts to detect alterations in the underlying tissue (a main method of detecting breast cancer).

**bulimia** An eating syndrome characterised by the alternation of binge eating and purging through such techniques as vomiting or use of laxatives.

**C fibre** Unmyelinated nerve fibres that respond to similar stimuli to A-delta fibres. Classically, they were considered to transmit dull, persistent or burning pain ('second pain').

**cardiovascular system** The transport system (heart, blood vessels and blood) of the body responsible for carrying oxygen and nutrients to the body and carrying away carbon dioxide and other wastes for excretion.

**Cartesian dualism** The seventeenth-century philosophical position advocating that mind (or soul) was separate from the body and that the body was mechanical and understood through physical and mathematical study.

**catecholamines** The neurotransmitters adrenaline and noradrenaline which promote sympathetic nervous system activity and are released in large amounts during stress.

**causalgia** Intense burning pain triggered by normally innocuous (harmless) stimuli.

**cholesterol** A fat-like material synthesised mainly in the liver and present in the blood and most tissues. High levels may be associated with heart disease and other disorders.

**chronic (pain/stress/disorders)** Illnesses or other disorders that occur over a long period of time and are usually not curable and therefore need to be managed.

**cognitive-behaviour therapy** Technique based on the principles from learning theory used to modify the cognitions and behaviours associated with some behaviour to be modified (e.g. smoking).

**coping** The process of trying to manage demands that are appraised as taxing or exceeding one's resources.

**coronary heart disease (CHD)** A general term referring to the illnesses caused by atherosclerosis (see above).

**cross-sectional studies** Studies involving different variables being measured at the same time as each other.

**cutaneous** Relating to the skin.

**diabetes** A chronic disorder in which the body is not able to manufacture or utilise insulin properly.

**efferent** Nerve impulses carried away from the central nervous system, outward towards the periphery (muscles, glands). Efferent neurones are also referred to as motor neurones.

**electrocardiogram (ECG)** Measure of heart rate activity.

**electroencephalogram (EEG)** Measure of the electrical activity of the brain.

**endocrine system** A system of ductless glands that secrete hormones directly into the blood to stimulate target organs (e.g. in response to stress). The endocrine system also interacts with nervous system functioning.

**epidemiology** The study of the frequency, distribution and causes of infectious and non-infectious diseases in a population based on an investigation of the physical and social environment.

**fight-or-flight response**  Pattern of physiological and bodily response that prepares the organism for an emergency.

**general adaptation syndrome (GAS)**  A three-phase profile of how an organism responds to stress, developed by Hans Selye.

**hardiness**  An individual difference characterised by a sense of commitment, a belief in personal control and a willingness to confront challenge. Believed to be a useful resource in coping with stressful events.

**health belief model**  A theory of health behaviour change based on perceived health threats and perceived effectiveness of actions in reducing such threats.

**health promotion**  A general philosophy that maintains that health is a personal and collective achievement and occurs through individual, social or policy initiatives.

**health psychology**  The sub-area within psychology devoted to the understanding of psychological influences on health and illness. It also considers the responses to these states, as well as the psychological origins and impacts of health policy and health interventions.

**helplessness**  The belief that one is powerless to effect change in one's environment. It may be considered as detrimental to a person's health.

**holistic (health/medicine)**  View that health is a positive state and a type of health/medicine focusing on treating the whole person (not simply the diseased part). Usually associated with certain non-traditional health practices.

**hypertension**  Excessively high blood pressure associated with a variety of medical problems, including coronary artery disease.

**hypothalamus**  That part of the forebrain responsible for regulating water balance and controlling hunger and sexual desire and the wider regulation of cardiac functioning, blood pressure, respiration and the endocrine system (see above).

**illness behaviour**  Activities undertaken by people who experience symptoms of illness, in order to find out more about their condition prior to visiting a doctor.

**immune system**  The body's resistance to injury from invading organisms, acquired from the mother at birth, through disease, or through inoculations.

**immunosuppression**  The degree to which the numbers of immune cells or their functioning are subdued (e.g. in response to stress).

**learned helplessness** Term used by Seligman (1975) to describe a learned passivity of response where patients learn that they cannot change the situation they are in. It may be considered as detrimental to a person's health (see also helplessness).

**locus of control** Belief about whether health events are controlled by one's self (internal) or the environment (external).

**lymph nodes** Filters through which lymph (fluid that bathes tissues, derived from the blood) passes in returning to the bloodstream.

**lymphatic system** The drainage system of the body, believed to be involved in immune functioning.

**mind–body relationship** The philosophical argument concerned with whether the mind and body operate indistinguishably as a single system or whether they act as two separate systems.

**morbidity** The number of cases of a disease that exist at some given point in time, expressed either as the number of new cases (incidence) or total number of existing cases (prevalence).

**mortality** The number of deaths due to particular causes.

**myelinated** Protein-based insulating layer around the axons of certain nerves.

**myocardial infarction** Heart attack produced when a clot has developed in a coronary vessel, blocking the flow of blood to the heart.

**neurone (nerve cell)** One of the basic functional units of the nervous system comprising a cell specialised to transmit electrical nerve impulses and so carry information from one part of the body to another.

**neurotransmitters** Chemicals involved in regulating nervous system functioning.

**nociceptors** Nerve cells that signal imminent or actual tissue damage.

**noradrenaline** A hormone closely related to **adrenaline**. Slows heart rate and increases rate and depth of breathing. Also released as a neurotransmitter substance by sympathetic nerve endings and implicated in the modification of pain in response to noxious stimuli.

**obesity** An excessive accumulation of body fat, believed to contribute to a variety of health disorders, including cardiovascular disease.

**operant conditioning** The rewarding (or punishment) of a response each time it occurs, so that in time it comes to occur more (or less) frequently.

**osteoporosis** A loss of bony tissue, resulting in bones that are brittle and likely to fracture.

**pathogen** A factor that compromises health. It is usually physical but may also be psychological or social in nature.

**phantom limb pain** Following amputation of a limb, the patient feels as if the limb still exists. The sensation of pain coming from the amputated part of the limb is known as 'phantom limb pain'.

**placebo** A medical treatment that has no active pharmacological properties but which may help to relieve a condition because of the patient's faith and expectation in its powers.

**primary appraisal** The perception of a new or changing event as negative, neutral or positive in response to stress.

**psychogenic** Having an origin in the mind rather than the body – a term usually applied to symptoms and illness.

**quality of life** The degree to which an individual is able to maximise his or her physical, psychological, vocational and social functioning.

**reappraisal** Terms used in coping with stress to describe a continual monitoring of a stressful response and our responses to it by making use of changing information as it becomes available.

**secondary appraisal** An assessment of one's own resources and coping abilities to meet perceived harm, threat or challenges in dealing with stress.

**self-image** An integrated set of beliefs about one's personal qualities and attributes.

**self-efficacy** The perception that one is able to perform a particular action.

**self-esteem** A global evaluation of one's qualities and attributes.

**serotonin** A neurotransmitter substance implicated in the process of sleep and the modification of pain in response to noxious stimuli.

**sick-role behaviour** Behaviour of people following a diagnosis, usually from a doctor, aimed at getting well.

**social support** Information from others that one is loved and cared for, esteemed and valued, and part of a network of communication and obligation.

**somatic nervous system** The somatic nervous system consists of all motor nerves that activate skeletal muscles and transmits messages arising from stimulation of the skin and muscles to the brain using sensory nerves.

**stress** A state that occurs when people encounter events that they perceive as endangering their physical or psychological well-being.

**stress responses** Reactions to events an individual perceives as endangering his or her well-being (e.g. see fight-or-flight response above).

**stressors** Events that an individual perceives as endangering his or her physical or psychological well-being.

**stroke** A condition that results from a disturbance in the blood flow to the brain, often marked by resulting physical or cognitive impairments and, in the extreme, death.

**sympathetic nervous system** The part of the nervous system that mobilises the body for action.

**T-cells (lymphocytes)** White blood cells that fight off infections within the immune system. They are responsible for cell-mediated immunity (in contrast to B-lymphocytes which are responsible for humoral immunity and circulate in the bloodstream).

**T-cells (transmission cells)** Cells in the dorsal horn of the spinal cord which control transmission of nociceptive (pain) information to the brain (not to be confused with T-cells in the immune system, above).

**testicular self-examination (TSE)** The practice of checking the testicles to detect alterations in the underlying tissue – a chief method of detecting early testicular cancer.

**unrealistic optimism** The belief that one is less vulnerable to a variety of adverse health events and more likely to incur a variety of positive events than is actually true.

**visceral organs** Organs within the body cavities, especially the organs of the abdominal cavities (stomach, intestines, etc.).

# Web-site addresses for additional information

### 1 The Society of Behavioural Medicine

http://psychweb.syr.edu/sbm/sisterorg.html

Extensive links to psychology sources, government sources and public health sites, including public health, psychology and medicine.

### 2 The Post-Traumatic Stress Resources Web Page

http://www.long-beach.va.gov/ptsd/stress.html

This web page lists and maintains information and links to professional information on Post-Traumatic Stress Syndrome.

### 3 Columbia University: Health and Stress (searchable data)

http:/www.alice.columbia.edu/

### 4 Stress

http://www.fisk.edu/vl/stress/

WWW virtual library on stress. Stress-related links, including commercial, government and non-profit web sites and resources.

## 5  On the lighter side . . . The Longevity Game

http://www.northwesternmutual.com/games/longevity/longevity-main.html

A game to determine how long one will live based on one's current style. Also listed as an activity in 4 (Stress) above.

## 6  University of York, UK

http://www.york.ac.uk

York University home page, leading into Psychology Department and extensive resources/links (including health psychology).

# Bibliography

Abrams, D., Abraham, C., Spears, R. and Marks, D. (1990) AIDS invulnerability: relationships, sexual behaviour and attitudes among 16–19-year-olds, in P. Aggleton, P. Davies and G. Hart (eds), *AIDS: Individual, Cultural and Policy Dimensions*, London: Falmer Press, 32–52.

American Psychiatric Association (APA) (1987) *Diagnostic and Statistical Manual of Mental Disorders*, 3rd rev. edn, Washington, DC: American Psychiatric Association.

Andrasik, F., Blanchard, E. B., Arena, J. G., Saunders, N. L. and Barron, K. D. (1982) Psychophysiology of recurrent headaches: methodological issues and new empirical findings, *Behaviour Therapy* 13, 407–29.

Atkinson, R. L., Atkinson, R. C., Smith, E. E. and Bem, D. (1993) *Introduction to Psychology*, 11th edn, New York: Harcourt Brace Jovanovich.

Bach, S., Noreng, M. F. and Tjellden, N. U. (1988) Phantom limb pain in amputees during the first 12-months following limb amputation after preoperative lumbar epidural blockade, *Pain* 33, 297–301.

Bain, D. J. G. (1977) Patient knowledge and the content of the consultation in general practice, *Medical Education* 11, 347–50.

Bandura, A. (1977) Self-efficacy, *Psychological Review* 84, 191–215.

Banyard, P. (1996) *Applying Psychology to Health*, London: Hodder and Stoughton.

Barber, T. X. (1984) Hypnosis, deep relaxation, and active relaxation: data, theory, and clinical applications, in R. L. Woolfolk and P. M. Lehrer (eds), *Principles and Practice of Stress Management*, New York: Guilford Press.

Becker, G. S. (1976) *The Economic Approach to Human Behavior*, Chicago: University of Chicago Press.

Beckman, H. B. and Frankel, R. M. (1984) The effect of physician behaviour on the collection of data, *Annals of Internal Medicine* 101, 692–6.

Beecher, H. K. (1956) Relationship of significance of wound to pain experienced, *Journal of the American Medical Association*, 161(17), 1609–13.

Belloc, N. B. and Breslow, L. (1972) Relationship of physical health status and health practices, *Preventative Medicine* 1, 409–21.

Bennett, P. and Murphy, S. (1997) *Psychology and Health Promotion*, Buckingham: Open University Press.

Benson, H. (1974) Your innate asset for combating stress, *Harvard Business Review* 52, 49–60.

Blanchard, E. B., Appelbaum, K. A., Radniz, C. L., Morrill, B., Michultka, D., Kirsch, C., Guarnieri, P., Attanasio, V., Andrasik, F., Jaccard, J. and Dentinger, M. P. (1990) Placebo-controlled evaluation of abbreviated progressive muscle relaxation and of relaxation combined with cognitive therapy in the treatment of tension headache, *Journal of Consulting and Clinical Psychology* 58, 210–15.

Bowling, A. (1997) *Measuring Health: A Review of Quality of Life Measurement Scales*. Buckingham: Open University Press.

Boyle, C. M. (1970) Differences between patients' and doctors' interpretations of common medical terms, *British Medical Journal* 2, 286–9.

Brannon, L. and Feist, J. (1997) *Health Psychology*, Pacific Grove, CA: Brooks Cole.

Budd, K. (1994) Monoamine function and analgesia, *Pain Reviews* 1(1), 3–8.

Cameron, L., Leventhal, E. A. and Leventhal, H. (1993) Symptom representations and affect as determinants of care seeking in a community-dwelling, adult sample population, *Health Psychology* 12, 171–9.

Carson, B. S. (1987) Neurologic and neurosurgical approaches to cancer pain, in D. B. McGuire and C. H. Yarbro (eds), *Cancer Pain Management*, Philadelphia: Saunders, 223–43.

Cave, S. (1999) *Therapeutic Approaches in Psychology*, London: Routledge.

Chapman, C. R. and Gunn, C. C. (1990) *Acupuncture*, in J. J. Bonica (ed.), *The Management of Pain*, 2nd edn, Malvern, PA: Lea and Febiger, 1805–21.

Clark, W. C. and Clark, S. B. (1980) Pain response in Nepalese porters, *Science* 209, 410–12.

Cooper, C. L. (1996) *Handbook of Stress, Medicine and Health*, London: CRC Press.

Cooper, K. H. (1982) *The Aerobics Program for Total Well-Being*, New York: Evans.

Crichton, E. F., Smith, D. L. and Demanuele, F. (1978) Patients' recall of medication information, *Drug Intelligence and Clinical Pharmacy* 12, 591–9.

Curtis, A. J. (1999) Understanding pain, *Psychology Review*, 6(1).

DiClemente, C. C., Prochaska, J. O., Fairhurst, S. K., Velicer, W. F., Velasquez, M. M. and Rossi, J. S. (1991) The process of smoking cessation: an analysis of precontemplation, contemplation, and preparation stages of change, *Journal of Consulting and Clinical Psychology* 59, 295–304.

Dolce, J. J. (1987) Self-efficacy and disability beliefs in behavioural treatment of pain, *Behaviour and Research Therapies* 25(4), 289–99.

Downie, R. S., Tannahill, C. and Tannahill, A. (1996) *Health Promotion: Models and Values*, Oxford: Oxford University Press.

Duby, G. (1993) *Love and Marriage in the Middle Ages*, London: Polity Press.

Ellis, A. (1962) *Reason and Emotion in Psychotherapy*, Secausus, NJ: Lyle Stuart.

Engel, G. L. (1977) The need for a new medical model: a challenge for biomedicine, *Science* 196, 129–35.

Evans, P., Clow, A. and Hucklebridge, F. (1997) Stress and the immune system, *The Psychologist* 10(7), 303–7.

Ewles, L. and Simnett, I. (1995) *Promoting Health: A Practical Guide*, London: Scutari Press.

Fallon, A. E. and Rozin, P. (1985) Sex differences in perceptions of desirable body shape, *Journal of Abnormal Psychology* 94, 102–5.

Fisher, S. and Reason, J. (1989) *Handbook of Life Stress, Cognition, and Health*, Chichester: Wiley.

Folkman, S. and Lazarus, R. S. (1988) *Manual for the Ways of Coping Questionnaire*, Palo Alto, CA: Consulting Psychologist Press.

Fordyce, W. E. (1974) Pain viewed as learned behavior, in J. J. Bonica (ed.), *Advances in Neurology*, vol. 4, New York: Raven.

—— (1976) *Behavioral Methods for Chronic Pain and Illness*, St Louis: Mosby.

Fraser, G. E., Beeson, W. L. and Phillips, R. L. (1991) Diet and lung cancer in California Seventh-day Adventists, *American Journal of Epidemiology* 133, 683–93.

Friedman, M. and Rosenman, R. H. (1959) Association of specific overt behavior pattern with blood and cardiovascular findings, *Journal of the American Medical Association* 169, 1286–97.

Friedman, M., Thoreson, C., Gill, J., Ulmer, D., Powell, L., Price, V., Brown, B., Thomson, L., Rabin, D., Breall, W., Bourg, E., Levy, R. and Dixon, T. (1986) Alteration of Type A behavior and its effects on cardiac reoccurrences in post myocardial infarction patients: summary results of the Recurrent Coronary Prevention Project, *American Heart Journal* 112, 653–65.

Fries, J. F., Green, L. W. and Levine, S. (1989) Health promotion and the compression of morbidity, *Lancet* 1, 481–3.

Garfinkel, P. E. and Garner, D. M. (1982) *Anorexia Nervosa: A Multidisciplinary perspective*, New York: Brunner-Mazel.

Garland, A. F. and Zigler, E. F. (1994) Psychological correlates of help-seeking attitudes among children and adolescents, *American Journal of Orthopsychiatry* 64, 586–93.

Glynn, C. J., Lloyd, J. W. and Folkard, S. (1981) Ventilatory responses to chronic pain, *Pain* 11, 201–12.

Greer, S., Morris, T. E. and Pettingale, K. W. (1979) Psychological responses to breast cancer: effect on outcome, *Lancet* 2, 785–7.

Hackett, T. P. and Weisman, A. D. (1969) Denial as a factor in patients with heart disease and cancer, *Annals of the New York Academy of Sciences* 164, 802–17.

Hamburg, D. A., Elliott, G. R. and Parron, D. L. (1982) *Health and Behavior: Frontiers of Research in the Behavioral Sciences*, Washington DC: National Academy Press.

Haynes, R. B., Sackett, D. L. and Taylor, D. W. (eds) (1979)

*Compliance in Health Care*, Baltimore, MD: Johns Hopkins University Press.

Hayward, S. (1998) Stress, health and psychoneuroimmunology, *Psychology Review* 5(1), 16–19.

Heuch, I., Kvale, G., Jacobsen, B. K. and Bjelke, E. (1983) Use of alcohol, tobacco and coffee, and risk of pancreatic cancer, *British Journal of Cancer* 48, 637–43.

Hilgard, E. R. (1979) Divided consciousness in hypnosis: the implications of the hidden observer, in E. Fromm and R. E. Shor (eds), *Hypnosis: Development in Research and New Perspectives*, Chicago: Aldine, 45–79.

Hilgard, E. R. and Hilgard, J. R. (1975) *Hypnosis in the Relief of Pain*, Los Altos, CA: Kauffman.

Hogan, J. (1989) Personality correlates of physical fitness, *Journal of Personality and Social Psychology* 56, 284–8.

Holland, W. W., Detels, R. and Knox, G. (eds) (1991) *Oxford Textbook of Public Health*, 2nd edn, Oxford: Oxford Medical Publications.

Homedes, N. (1991) Do we know how to influence patients' behaviour?, *Family Practice* 8(4), 412–23.

Hongladrom, T. and Hongladrom, G. C. (1982) The problem of testicular cancer: how health professionals in the armed services can help, *Military Medicine* 147, 211–13.

Hyland, M. E. and Kenyon, C. A. P. (1992) A measure of positive health-related quality of life: the Satisfaction with Illness Scale, *Psychological Reports*, 71, 1137–38.

Jachuk, S. J., Brierly, H., Jachuck, S. and Willcox, P. M. (1982) The effect of hypotensive drugs on the quality of life, *Journal of the Royal College of General Practitioners* 32, 103–5.

Jacobs, T. J. and Charles, E. (1980) Life events and the occurrence of cancer in children, *Psychosomatic Medicine* 42, 11–24.

Jacobson, E. (1934) *You Must Relax*, New York: McGraw-Hill.

—— (1938) *Progressive Relaxation: A Physiological and Clinical Investigation of Muscle States and their Significance in Psychology and Medical Practice*, 2nd edn, Chicago: University of Chicago Press.

Johnson, C. and Larson, R. (1982) Bulimia: an analysis of moods and behaviour, *Psychosomatic Medicine* 44, 341–51.

Kabat-Zinn, J., Lipworth, L. and Burney, R. (1985) The clinical use of mindfulness meditation for the self-regulation of chronic pain, *Journal of Behavioral Medicine* 8, 163–90.

Karasek, R. and Theorell, T. (1990) *Healthy Work: Stress, Productivity and the Reconstruction of Working Life*, New York: Basic Books.

Kasl, S. V. and Cobb, S. (1966a) Health behavior, illness behavior, and sick role behavior I. Health and illness behavior, *Archives of Environmental Health* 12, 246–66.

—— (1966b) Health behavior, illness behavior, and sick role behavior II. Sick role behavior, *Archives of Environmental Health* 12, 531–41.

Kelly, W. D. and Friesen, S. (1950) Do cancer patients want to be told?, *Surgery* 27, 822–6.

Kiselica, M. S., Baker, S. B., Thomas, R. N. and Reedy, S. (1994) Effects of stress inoculation training on anxiety, stress, and academic performance among adolescents, *Journal of Counselling Psychology* 41, 335–42.

Klohn, L. S. and Rogers, R. W. (1991) Dimensions of the severity of a health threat: the persuasive effects of visibility, time of onset, and rate of onset in young women's intentions to prevent osteoporosis, *Health Psychology* 10, 323–9.

Kobasa, S. C. (1979) Stressful life events and health: an enquiry into hardiness, *Journal of Personality and Social Psychology* 37, 1–11.

Kobasa, S. C., Maddi, S. R. and Puccetti, M. C. (1982) Personality and exercise as buffers in the stress–illness relationship, *Journal of Behavioral Medicine* 5, 391–404.

Koniak-Griffin, D. (1994) Aerobic exercise, psychological well-being, and physical discomforts during adolescent pregnancy, *Research in Nursing and Health* 17, 253–68.

Kremer, E. F., Atkinson, J. H., Jr. and Ignelzi, R. J. (1981) Pain measurement: the affective dimensional measure of the McGill Pain Questionnaire with a cancer pain population, *Pain* 12, 153–63.

Kubler-Ross, E. (1969) *On Death and Dying*, New York: Macmillan.

Kuczmarski, R. J. (1992) Prevalence of overweight and weight gain in the United States, *American Journal of Clinical Nutrition* 55, 495–502.

Kuntzleman, C. T. (1978) *Rating the Exercise*, New York: Morrow.

Lakka, T. A., Venalainen, J. M., Rauramaa, R., Salonen, R.,

Tuomilehto, J. and Salonen, J. T. (1994) Relations of leisure-time physical activity and cardiorespiratory fitness to the risk of acute myocardial infarction in men. *New England Journal of Medicine* 330, 1549–54.

Lazarus, R. S. and Folkman, S. (1984) *Stress, Appraisal, and Coping*, New York: Springer.

Leiderman, D. B. and Grisso, J. A. (1985) The Gomer phenomenon, *Journal of Health and Social Behavior* 25, 222–32.

Lerner, R. M. and Gellert, E. (1969) Body build identification, preference and aversion in children, *Developmental Psychology* 1, 456–62.

Leventhal, H. and Diefenbach, M. (1991) The active side of illness cognition, in J. A. Skelton and R. T. Croyle (eds), *Mental Representation in Health and Illness*, New York: Springer-Verlag, 247–72.

Ley, P. (1981) Professional non-compliance: a neglected problem, *British Journal of Clinical Psychology* 20, 151–4.

—— (1982) Giving information to patients, in J. R. Eiser (ed.), *Social Psychology and Behavioural Science*, Chichester: Wiley.

—— (1988) *Communicating with Patients*, London: Croom Helm.

—— (1989) Improving patients' understanding, recall, satisfaction and compliance, in S. Rachman (ed.), *Contributions to Medical Psychology*, Oxford: Pergamon Press, 117–49.

McKeown, T. (1979) *The Role of Medicine*, Oxford: Blackwell.

MacWhinney, D. R. (1973) Problem-solving and decision making in primary medical practice. *Proceedings of the Royal Society of Medicine* 65, 934–8.

Marcus, B. H., Radowski, W. and Rossi, J. S. (1992) Assessing motivational readiness and decision-making for exercise, *Health Psychology* 22, 3–16.

Mason, J. W. (1975) A historical view of the stress field. Pt. 2, *Journal of Human Stress* 1, 22–36.

Matarazzo, J. D. (1994) Health and behaviour: the coming-together of science and practice in psychology and medicine after a century of benign neglect, *Journal of Clinical Psychology in Medical Settings* 1, 7–39.

Mechanic, D. (1978) *Medical Sociology*, 2nd edn, New York: Free Press.

Mehta, M. and Wynn-Parry, C. B. (1994) Mechanical back pain

and the facet joint syndrome, *Disability and Rehabilitation: An International Multidisciplinary Journal* 16(1), 2–12.

Meichenbaum, D. and Cameron, R. (1983) Stress inoculation training: toward a general paradigm for training coping skills, in D. Meichenbaum and M. E. Jaremko (eds), *Stress Reduction and Prevention*, New York: Plenum, 115–54.

Melzack, R. (1975) The McGill Pain Questionnaire: major properties and scoring methods, *Pain* 1, 277–99.

—— (1987) The short-form McGill Pain Questionnaire, *Pain* 30, 191–7.

—— (1992) Phantom limbs, *Scientific American*, April, 90–6.

Melzack, R. and Wall, P. D. (1965) Pain mechanisms – a new theory, *Science* 150, 971–9.

—— (1982) *The Challenge of Pain*, New York: Basic Books.

—— (1991) *The Challenge of Pain*, rev. edn, London: Penguin.

Melzack, R., Wall, P. D. and Ty, T. C. (1982) Acute pain in an emergency clinic: latency of onset and descriptor patterns, *Pain* 14, 33–43.

Merskey, H., Albe-Fessard, D. G., Bonica, J. J., Carmen, A., Dubner, R., Kerr, F. W. L., Lindblom, U., Mumford, J. M., Nathan, P. W., Noordenbos, W., Pagni, C. A., Renaer, M. J., Sternbach, R. A. and Sunderland, S. (1979) IASP sub-committee on taxonomy, *Pain* 6(3), 249–52.

Miller, N. E. (1969) Learning of visceral and glandular responses, *Science* 163, 434–45.

Milner, P. (1997) *Health and Deprivation in Rural Areas*, Annual Report of the Director of Public Health, Wiltshire Health Authority.

Morris, J. N., Heady, J. A., Raffle, P. A. B., Roberts, C. G. and Parks, J. W. (1953) Coronary heart-disease and physical activity of work, *Lancet*, ii, 1053–57, 1111–20.

Murray, M. and Macmillan, C. (1993) Health beliefs, locus of control, emotional control and women's cancer screening behaviour, *British Journal of Clinical Psychology* 32, 87–100.

National Cancer Institute (1987) *1986 Annual Cancer Statistics Review* (NIH publication No. 87–2789), Bethesda, MD: National Institutes of Health.

National Center for Health Statistics (1992) *Vital Statistics of the United States (1992)*, Washington, DC: US Government Printing Office.

Nelson, T. S. and Planchock, N. Y. (1989) The effects of trans-cutaneous electrical nerve stimulation (TENS) on postoperative patients' pain and narcotic use, in S. G. Funk, E. M. Tornquist, M. T. Champagne, L. A. Copp and R. A. Wiese (eds), *Key Aspects of Comfort: Management of Pain, Fatigue, and Nausea*, New York: Springer, 134–45.

Nielson, J. and Arendt-Nielson, L. (1997) Spatial summation of heat induced pain within and between dermatomes, *Somatosensory and Motor Research* 14(2), 119–25.

Norvell, N. and Belles, D. (1993) Psychological and physical benefits of weight training in law enforcement personnel, *Journal of Consulting and Clinical Psychology* 61, 520–7.

Ogden, J. (1996) *Health Psychology: A Textbook*, Buckingham: Open University Press.

Orne, M. T. (1980) Hypnotic control of pain: toward a clarification of the different psychological processes involved, in J. J. Bonica (ed.), *Pain*, New York: Raven, 155–72.

*Our Healthier Nation: A Contract for Health*, London Stationery Office, 1998.

Paffenbarger, R. S., Jr., Wing, A. L. and Hyde, R. T. (1978) Physical activity as an index of heart attack risk in college alumni, *American Journal of Epidemiology* 108, 1109–14.

Pennebaker, J. W. (1982) *The Psychology of Physical Symptoms*, New York: Springer-Verlag.

Pierce, E. F. and Pate, D. W. (1994) Mood alterations in older adults following acute exercise, *Perceptual and Motor Skills* 79, 191–4.

Pike, K. M. and Rodin, J. (1991) Mothers, daughters, and disordered eating, *Journal of Abnormal Psychology* 100, 1–7.

Pinder, K. L., Ramirez, A. J., Black, M. E., Richards, M. A., Gregory, W. M. and Rubens, R. D. (1993) Psychiatric disorder in patients with advanced breast cancer: prevalence and associated factors, *European Journal of Cancer* 29A, 524–7.

Pipes, T. V. and Wilmore, J. H. (1975) Isokinetic vs. isotonic strength training in adult men, *Medical Science Sports* 7, 262–74.

Pitts, M. and Phillips, K. (eds) (1998) *Health Psychology: An Introduction*, London: Routledge.

Prochaska, J. O. and DiClemente, C. C. (1982) Transtheoretical therapy: toward a more integrative model of change, *Psychotherapy: Theory, Research and Practice* 19, 276–88.

Prochaska, J. O., DiClemente, C. C. and Norcross, J. C. (1992) In search of how people change: applications to addictive behaviours, *American Psychologist* 47, 1102–14.

Prochaska, T. R., Keller, U. L., Leventhal, E. A. and Leventhal, H. (1987) Impact of symptoms and aging attribution on emotions and coping, *Health Psychology* 6, 495–514.

Rakoff, V. (1983) Multiple determinants of family dynamics in anorexia, in P. L. Darby, P. E. Garfinkel, D. M. Garner and D. V. Coscina (eds), *Anorexia Nervosa: Recent Developments in Research*, New York: Liss, 29–40.

Reynolds, P. M., Sanson-Fisher, R. W., Poole, A. D., Harker, J. and Byrne, M. J. (1981) Cancer and communication: information-givinig in an oncology clinic, *British Medical Journal* 282: 1449–51.

Rosenstock, I. M. (1966) Why people use health services, *Millbank Memorial Fund Quarterly* 44, 94–124.

Ross, C. E. and Hayes, D. (1988) Exercise and psychologic well-being in the community, *American Journal of Epidemiology* 127, 762–71.

Roth, H. P. (1979) Problems in conducting a study of the effects of patient compliance of teaching the rationale for antacid therapy, in S. J. Cohen (ed.), *New Directions in Patient Compliance*, Lexington, MA: Lexington Books, 111–26.

Roth, D. L. and Holmes, D. S. (1985) Influence of physical fitness in deterring the impact of stressful life events on physical and psychologic health, *Psychosomatic Medicine* 47, 164–73.

Royal College of General Practitioners (1972) *The Future General Practitioner*, RCGP.

Ruuskanen, J. M. and Parkatti, T. (1994) Physical activity and related factors among nursing home residents, *Journal of the American Geriatrics Society* 42, 987–91.

Sarafino, (1994) *Health Psychology: Biopsychosocial Interactions*, Chichester: Wiley.

Seligman, M. E. P. (1975) *Helplessness: On Depression, Development and Death*, San Francisco: Freeman.

Selye, H. (1956) *The Stress of Life*, New York: McGraw-Hill.

—— (1982) History and present status of the stress concept, in L. Goldberger and S. Breznitz (eds), *Handbook of Stress: Theoretical and Clinical Aspects*, New York: Free Press, 7–17.

Shaffer, J. W., Graves, P. L., Swank, R. T. and Pearson, T. A. (1987) Clustering of personality traits in youth and the subsequent development of cancer among physicians, *Journal of Behavioral Medicine* 10, 441–7.

Shekelle, R. B., Rossof, A. H. and Stamler, J. (1991) Dietary cholesterol and incidence of lung cancer: the Western Electric study, *American Journal of Epidemiology* 134, 480–4.

Siegel, P. Z., Brackbill, R. M. and Heath, G. W. (1995) The epidemiology of walking for exercise: implications for promoting activity among sedentary groups, *American Journal of Public Health* 85, 706–10.

Silber, J. (1999) *The Physiology of Behaviour*, London: Routledge.

Simone, C. B. (1983) *Cancer and Nutrition*, New York: McGraw-Hill.

Simonton, O. C. and Simonton, S. S. (1975) Belief systems and the management of emotional aspects of malignancy, *Journal of Transpersonal Psychology* 7, 29–47.

Sinyor, D., Golden, M., Steinert, Y. and Seraganian, P. (1986) Experimental manipulation of aerobic fitness and the response to psychosocial stress: heart rate and self-report measures, *Psychosomatic Medicine* 48, 324–37.

Skevington, S. M. (1995) *The Psychology of Pain*, Chichester: Wiley.

Smith, A. and Jacobson, B. (1989) *The Nation's Health*, London: The King's Fund.

Sodroski, J. G., Rosen, C. A. and Haseltine, W. A. (1984) Transacting transcription of the long terminal repeat of human T lymphocyte viruses in infected cells, *Science* 225, 381–5.

Solomon, G. F. and Temoshok, L. (1987) A psychoneuroimmunologic perspective on AIDS research: questions, preliminary findings, and suggestions, *Journal of Applied Social Psychology* 17, 286–308.

Solomon, G. F., Temoshok, L., O'Leary, A. and Zich, J. A. (1987) An intensive psychoimmunologic study of long-surviving persons with AIDS: pilot work, background studies, hypotheses, and methods, *Annals of the New York Academy of Sciences* 46, 647–55.

Sonstroem, R. J. (1984) Exercise and self-esteem, *Exercise and Sport Sciences Reviews* 12, 123–55.

Stainton-Rogers, W. (1991) *Explaining Health and Illness: An*

*Exploration of Diversity*, Hemel Hempstead: Harvester Wheatsheaf.

Stroebe, W. and Stroebe, M. (1995) *Social Psychology and Health*, Buckingham: Open University Press.

Stunkard, A. J. (1984) The current status of treatment for obesity in adults, in A. J. Stunkard and E. Stellar (eds), *Eating and its Disorders*, New York: Raven Press.

Suchman, E. A. (1965) Social patterns of illness and medical care, *Journal of Health and Human Behavior* 6, 2–16.

Syrjala, K. L. and Chapman, C. R. (1984) Measurement of clinical pain: a review and integration of research findings, in C. Benedetti, C. R. Chapman and G. Mooricca (eds), *Advances in Pain Research and Therapy*, Vol. 7. *Recent Advances in the Management of Pain*, New York: Raven.

Szabo, S., Orley, J. and Saxena, S. (1997) An approach to response scale development for cross-cultural questionnaires. *European Psychologist* 2(3) September, 270–6.

Taylor, S. E. (1983) Adjustment to threatening events: a theory of cognitive adaptation, *American Psychologist* 38, 1161–73.

—— (1995) *Health Psychology*, 3rd edn, New York: McGraw-Hill.

Thompson, S. C. and Pitts, J. S. (1992) In sickness and in health: chronic illness, marriage and spousal caregiving, in S. Spacapan and S. Oskamp (eds), *Helping and Being Helped: Naturalistic Studies*, Newbury Park, CA: Sage, 115.

Toniolo, P., Riboli, E., Protta, F., Charrel, M. and Coppa, A. P. (1989) Calorie-providing nutrients and risk of breast cancer, *Journal of the National Cancer Institute* 81, 278–86.

Turk, D. C., Meichenbaum, D. and Genest, M. (1983) *Pain and Behavioral Medicine: A Cognitive Behavioral Perspective*, New York: Guilford Press.

Turner, J. A. and Chapman, C. R. (1982a) Psychological interventions for chronic pain: a critical review. I: Relaxation training and biofeedback, *Pain* 12, 1–21.

—— (1982b) Psychological interventions for chronic pain: a critical review. II: Operant conditioning, hypnosis, and cognitive-behavior therapy, *Pain* 12, 23–46.

Van der Does, A. J. and Van Dyck, R. (1989) Does hypnosis contribute to the care of burn patients? Review of evidence, *General Hospital Psychiatry* 11, 119–24.

van der Ploeg, J. M., Vervest, H. A. M., Liem, A. L. and Schagen van Leeuwen, J. H. (1996) Transcutaneous nerve stimulation (TENS) during the first stage of labour: a randomized clinical trial, *Pain* 68, 75–8.

Verbrugge, L. M. (1989) The twain meet: empirical explanation of sex differences in health and mortality, *Journal of Health and Social Behavior* 24, 16–30.

Verrault, R., Brisson, J., Deschenes, L., Naud, F., Meyer, F. and Balanger, L. (1988) Dietary fat in relation to prognostic indicators of breast cancer, *Journal of the National Cancer Institute* 80, 819–25.

Wadden, T. A. and Brownell, K. D. (1984) The development and modification of dietary practices in individuals, groups and large populations, in J. D. Matarazzo and S. M. Weiss (eds), *Behavioural Health: A Handbook of Health Enhancement and Disease Prevention*, New York: Wiley.

Weinman, J. (1987) Diagnosis as problem-solving, in *An Outline of Psychology as Applied to Medicine*, 2nd edn, London: Wright.

Weinstein, N. (1984) Why it won't happen to me: perceptions of risk factors and susceptibility, *Health Psychology* 3, 431–57.

WHO (World Health Organization) (1946) *Constitution*, New York: WHO.

—— (1993) *Doctor–Patient Interaction and Communication*, Geneva: WHO.

WHOQUOL Group (World Health Organization Quality of Life Group) (1993) Study protocol for the World Health Organization project to develop a quality of life assessment instrument (WHOQUOL), *Quality of Life Research* 2, 153–9.

Wolf, S. L., Nacht, M. and Kelly, J. L. (1982) EMG feedback training during dynamic movement for low back pain patients, *Behavior Therapy* 13, 395–406.

# Index

# Routledge Modular Psychology

Series editors: Cara Flanagan is the Assessor for the Associated Examining Board (AEB) and an experienced A-level author. Kevin Silber is Senior Lecturer in Psychology at Staffordshire University. Both are A-level examiners in the UK.

The *Routledge Modular Psychology* series is a completely new approach to introductory level psychology, tailor-made to the new modular style of teaching. Each short book covers a topic in more detail than any large textbook can, allowing teacher and student to select material exactly to suit any particular course or project.

The books have been written especially for those students new to higher-level study, whether at school, college or university. They include specially designed features to help with technique, such as a model essay at an average level with an examiner's comments to show how extra marks can be gained. The authors are all examiners and teachers at the introductory level.

The *Routledge Modular Psychology* texts are all user-friendly and accessible and include the following features:

- sample essays with specialist commentary to show how to achieve a higher grade
- chapter summaries to assist with revision
- progress and review exercises
- glossary of key terms
- summaries of key research
- further reading to stimulate ongoing study and research
- website addresses for additional information
- cross-referencing to other books in the series

y TI

ology

*Health Psychology* is a lively and refreshing introduction to the contribution psychology has made to our understanding of health. Anthony J. Curtis begins by defining health psychology and describes the main theoretical models which underpin it. He then considers the additional fields of social epidemiology and health policy. Pain and pain management, doctor–patient communication, psychological factors in illness, the impact of lifestyles on health, and stress and stress management are all discussed. Psychological theory is applied to health psychology practice throughout to show the relevance of theories, models and health psychology research to everyday health behaviours.

*Health Psychology* is tailor-made for the student new to higher-level study. With its helpful textbook features provided to assist in examination and learning techniques, it should interest all intro-ductory psychology students, as well as those training for the caring services, whether nurses, paramedics or social workers.

**Anthony J. Curtis** is a Senior Lecturer in Psychology at Bath Spa University College, a former Team Leader for A-Level psychology and Senior Editor for *Psychology Review*.